T0301814

THE CASE FOR CASES:
Teaching with Cases

How to Teach Using the Case Method

THE CASE FOR CASES:
Teaching with Cases

How to Teach Using the Case Method

Philip Zerrillo

Singapore Management University, Singapore

 **World Scientific**

NEW JERSEY · LONDON · SINGAPORE · BEIJING · SHANGHAI · HONG KONG · TAIPEI · CHENNAI · TOKYO

Published by

World Scientific Publishing Co. Pte. Ltd.

5 Toh Tuck Link, Singapore 596224

USA office: 27 Warren Street, Suite 401-402, Hackensack, NJ 07601

UK office: 57 Shelton Street, Covent Garden, London WC2H 9HE

British Library Cataloguing-in-Publication Data
A catalogue record for this book is available from the British Library.

THE CASE FOR CASES: TEACHING WITH CASES
How to Teach Using the Case Method

ISBN 978-981-3273-34-4

For any available supplementary material, please visit
https://www.worldscientific.com/worldscibooks/10.1142/11073#t=suppl

Desk Editor: Sandhya Venkatesh

Typeset by Stallion Press
Email: enquiries@stallionpress.com

Printed in Singapore

ACKNOWLEDGEMENTS

Those who can, do. Those who teach truly shape the future.

In writing a book such as this, there are so many people to thank. For me, this journey would not have been possible without my family, my professional colleagues and, of course, the faculty that inspired me to find my voice in the classroom.

I want to thank my mother and father, Mary Ellen and Edward Zerrillo, for their support and the love and affection that they provided to all of their six children. To those brothers and sisters, Ed Jr, Daniel, Bonnie, Ellen and Niki, thanks so much. Each of you had a hand in this.

To my wife (Karen) and two sons, Philip Jr. (PEZ) and Michael, this is for you, as like all of my work, is truly a family experience.

It is with the deepest admiration and respect that I want to thank my colleagues at the Singapore Management University Centre for Management Practice. Each of you in your own way has helped this book to be possible. To the "Amazing Irene Soh," thanks for keeping me between the lines. You are truly the one that enables all of us hit our goals and targets each year. Adina Wong, your support and persistence is inspirational. Lipika Bhattacharya, your calm, pleasant demeanor and sheer level of effort is a standard for anyone to strive towards. Thank you Alvin Lee for your solid unwavering delivery. To Sheila, thank you for teaching me about crops, bleeds, pagination and all other publishing issues. To Suh Wen, for your organization and incredible speed when a task arises. Thank you to our writers Sheetal Bhardwaj, Sarita Mathur and Chan Chi Wei for teaching me what "well written" really means. And, of course, Havovi Joshi who has always been a great encouragement and a trusted confidant during the highs and lows of writing a book like this.

Most of all, this is a book that is meant to be a "thank you" to my teachers and those who taught with me how to teach, often without knowing it. I want to start with Dawn Iacobucci, who was always a part of our lives as doctoral students. To Dipak Jain, who taught me so many of the tools I use to this day. Thanks to Lou Stern, who showed me that you never short the kids on what you are delivering as today may be the day that you inspire someone to do something great. For Eyal Maoz, who is one of the finest teachers I have ever met and who was always happy to share his thoughts as we both learned how to teach.

To the Texas gang, I want to thank Raj Srivastava my first department chairman, my often co-instructor Tassu Shervani who provided me fabulous insights into how to create your personality in the classroom, and some of our doctoral students Goutam Challagalla and Shantanu Bhattacharya (that skinny young PhD student who 25 years later was my colleague at SMU) I can't thank you all enough.

And, of course, the story would not be complete without thanking the folks I taught with at SMU. Thanks to Tan Chin Tiong, Srini Reddy, Kapil Tuli and Themin Suwardy for your support, wisdom and classroom excellence. You served as both an inspiration and a yardstick to measure my progress against.

One final group of faculty deserves special note. As I moved into my early 50's, I began teaching with three outstanding teachers — Professors Court Huber, James Nolan and John Daily. Teaching together, with each of us observing and adding to one another's comments was energizing and eye opening. Few faculty have the patience to watch others teach. Still fewer are willing to share the stage with others of fantastic intellect. I would dare say this was an experience that helped me to go beyond what I was individually capable of.

And to the many students that I have had over these past 30 years: Thanks for your patience, your contributions and your comments. I could have never gotten here without your preparation, contributions and feedback.

Thank you all.

PROLOGUE

This book is meant for all of those that come to work each day and inspire the next generation of learners. Through the years, I have come to learn that even what appears to be the most spontaneous of classroom interactions can be sparked, shaped and directed with proper planning, forethought and practice. I hope that this book will help you to find the teaching style that works best for you, your students and the material that you need to teach.

Whether you teach at a research institution or a polytechnic, much of your work life experience will be determined by your ability to perform in the classroom. Your classroom experiences can lead to the best of days and unfortunately some of the most soul searching times as you try to understand what went wrong. Hopefully, this book will lead to better days ahead.

CONTENTS

Chapter 1

INTRODUCTION: THE CASE FOR CASES

Why Use Cases? *The educational value!*

There are many ways to teach a class and some are more appropriate than others for different levels of students and different types of material. The pedagogical value of all types of teaching can be debated, but there are a number of clear advantages that case teaching has when compared to other formats.

Real life

First and foremost, case teaching is a way of transporting the student from a classroom to a quasi-real-life situation. By placing students in a real-life scenario (be it an authentic management problem or a fictional case that represents an amalgamation of real firm problems), cases are an opportunity to move out of the classroom and closer to the problems that "would-be practitioners" will confront.

Relevance

Case problems and case teaching can add a degree of relevance and authenticity to your teaching. By providing real-life problems faced by business practitioners, the students are able to envision the career decisions and management challenges they might face. Learning about how managers are given information and the way in which they must analyze data and make decisions provides an opportunity for students to visualize and understand *"the real world."* Cases allow for the students to begin understanding the pressures, challenges and trade-offs that managers must make as they attempt to ply their trade.

Active learning

Case teaching transports the educational experience from passive to active learners. In a typical classroom setting, students passively receive the message of the lecturer. While good teachers are able to craft their messages to connect with the student's internal mental dialogue, the process does not offer a great opportunity for the customized learning that comes with interactive participation. Students are merely recipients of these well-crafted messages. Similarly, when reading books and course materials, there is often an intention on the student's part to memorize the same rather than actively apply the concepts to the problem at hand. The case setting, whether it is a class discussion or an assignment, demands that the students actively participate in solving a problem.[1]

More and more fields are starting to recognize the benefits of specifically case teaching, and more broadly active learning. Indeed, even those instructing in the sciences have been questioning the value of the sage on the stage, or a stand and deliver method of delivering. Often with massive lecture halls and inattentive audiences, the sciences have begun to find that there are tremendous benefits in these pedagogies (see **Box Story 1**).

---

[1] For more, see Leslie Sharkey, Jed Overmann and Pamela Flash 2007 as they extol the virtues of using a case method for teaching veterinary pathology.

Recognition and problem solving skills

As students put forth solutions to case problems, they begin to learn how to break complex issues into solvable problems. In speaking with one of the Harvard case teaching trainers, he was adamant that by the time a student is finished analyzing 100 or so cases in their MBA programme, they should be better at spotting problems, and finding potential levers and supporting arguments to solve them.

Decision making

One of the most sought after skills among employers is finding graduates that can "make decisions." Indeed, a 2008 Mercer study reports that decision-making ability is "a top three reason why firms hire." The case study method of teaching represents an ideal opportunity to force the students to make decisions. The presentation and teaching of a case itself demands a reasonable solution from the students. Thus they must make decisions as to what is the appropriate course of action to solve the problem at hand.

Awareness of the ethical perils of decisions

Voicing one's solutions and the steps that one might take to achieve them provides students with an opportunity to have their decisions and solutions critiqued by their peers. This can reduce the potential of unethical decision-making, or even decisions that extend beyond the norms of society. Faculty teaching controversial topics such as human genetics have extolled the virtues of teaching analytic skills through the case method.[2] Having 50 or 100 peers comment on your approach in a classroom is greatly preferred to unleashing would-be decision makers into their trade only to find

---

[2] Lundeberg, M, K Mogen; M Bergland; K Klyczek, Journal of College Science Teaching;

that they have not been trained to consider the ethical challenges or social norms that will be applied.

Informal presentation skills

One of the greatest, but least recognized, benefits of the case method is the ability to learn informal presentation skills. The inquisitive teaching method helps students to answer spontaneous questions in front of an audience. Over time, the student's inhibition to answer questions in front of others declines. Their confidence to present their thoughts and accompanying reasons improves, and this creates a very different graduate, comfortable in participating and sharing.

A Personal Insight

I began my teaching career in the West and I was accustomed to primarily American students that would gladly contribute their thoughts (sometimes with little preparation) in class discussions. I also noticed that the East Asian and South East Asian students did not readily offer their insights. As I began working in ASEAN, I found that this lack of contribution to the discussion was actually limiting the graduate's career progression. Despite being capable, talented and well trained, these students were not progressing in the multinational (MNC) workplace. Managers need human talent that can follow directions, make decisions, and most of all, contribute to the management, strategy and direction of the organization when called upon. That is, they want people that can stand up and share their thoughts, and in a group-discussion, add to the insights. This disclosure and contribution to the planning and execution of work is taken by managers to be a sign of employees that are committed and taking responsibility. Conversely, students that are unwilling to share are often suspected of being uncommitted, unprepared or worse yet incapable.

This lack of career progression and skills gap was a primary driver in the establishment of Singapore Management University, and promoting the use of the case methodology in the classroom.

Tan Chin Tiong, Ph.D., founding Provost, and Professor of Marketing at Singapore Management University explained,

We sought to create a different student. We wanted to produce graduates that were comfortable contributing in meetings and offering their experience, wisdom and insights. The case methodology was a key ingredient in creating this personality among our graduates. Sharing their views in the classroom for several years prepares them for the management meetings that they will encounter as they leave this university. We find that employers constantly come back to the university staff and say, "your students are different! We like them, they have a can-do spirit that is hard for us to find." Frankly, the case method is a big part of what helps our students to feel confident in sharing and stepping up.

In my own teaching career, I have noticed the dramatic evolution in soft-skills among students at case-based universities. Knowing how to add to class discussion, while often having to go beyond or be critical of their peers, is an important management skill. Being able to contribute, add to, or disagree with others in a public setting is a talent that helps graduates learn, improvise and contribute in the workplace. In direct comparison, students that sit in the back of a lecture hall watching the back of another student's head generally struggle with how to challenge other's thoughts, or add to the discussion without appearing rude. Having to exhibit logic, in a polite, spontaneous and diplomatic manner is in large part a key to a successful career.

Additionally, as students participate in class discussion and listen to their peers make contributions, they become better thinkers and better communicators. When other students get a better answer and get it quicker, their classmates are forced to ask the internal questions of: "How did they get that answer? And what did they do or know that I don't?" As the instructor drills down on the student's logic, assumptions and instincts, the others learn new and different arguments and problem solving skills. This open and free discussion is essential in breaking down the students' preconceived notions of how to solve problems and teaches them more, different, and potentially better problem solving skills. ***This point cannot be understated, as many of the jobs our students will work at in 10 years have not yet been created. We need to prepare problem-solvers for all seasons.***

But, not all students offer good answers. As a matter of fact, students can often provide very poor solutions with weak arguments that often seem disconnected from the problem at hand. Students watching and listening to this discussion and the way that the instructor deals with these answers can help students to be better communicators. That is, they often observe that their high achieving peers can easily misunderstand seemingly obvious content and fall into logic traps that were not obvious to others. This helps students that experience the case method to understand where questions and logic can go astray or "off the rails." Witnessing such classroom tragedies helps make students better communicators as they begin to understand how simple concepts can be misunderstood by even the brightest of colleagues.

From the previous discussion, it would appear that the merits of case teaching seem to be strong and apparent. Indeed, in a study conducted in 2006 by the US-based National Center for Case Study Teaching in Science, a sample of 101 faculty were asked why instructors for the case method should use the case method for their students, and they replied in much the same manner as what we see above.[3]

In classes using the case study method, students:

a) Demonstrate stronger critical thinking skills (88.8%)
b) Make connections across multiple content areas (82.6%)
c) Develop a deeper understanding of concepts (90.1%)
d) Are better able to view an issue from multiple perspectives (91.3%)
e) Take a more active part in class (95.1%)
f) Are more engaged (93.8%)
g) Develop positive peer-to-peer relationships (80.1)

The Perils of Teaching with Cases?

While these first seven questions paint quite a rosy picture thus far, it should be noted that faculty also reported:

h) Students evaluate my teaching more positively: 45%

Despite all of the potential benefits, it seems that there is no strong student evaluation-based reason for adopting the case method. Indeed, slightly more than half of the instructors believe that their course is *not* evaluated more favorably.

Why is this? Do students not see the benefits of case teaching? Several answers come to mind. In my 25 years of teaching, I have noted that students most often make the following five complaints.

---

[3] Lundeberg, *et al.* (2007). National survey of faculty perceptions of the benefits and challenges of using case studies. JCST, 34–37.

1) "I don't know how to prepare for class".
   Being prepared for a class discussion takes time and effort. Unlike browsing through a chapter or handout and then waiting for the professor to lecture, case participants must be ready to answer questions — often in a lightning fast manner. In a case-based class, students spend a great deal of time outside of their comfort zone. They can no longer sit in the classroom, watching their faculty bring their greatest thoughts, energy and passion to the stage. Instead, they have to now supply their logic, insights and theoretical understanding of the facts and environment. It is quite obvious what would be easier for all students.

2) "Others monopolize the discussion." Or equally likely, "I am shy and don't want to talk."
   The case teacher must be aware that there is a democracy in the classroom and all of the students need to participate. One of the skills we will work on in this book is how to get the shy and the reticent to contribute. Another skill to be addressed is how to limit the over-zealous. That is, those that often hijack a good discussion and turn it into a dialogue that freezes others out.

3) "Some people just say anything. It is often stupid and irrelevant."
   Your job and skill as an instructor will not only be to get students to talk, but to ensure there are standards set for the quality of content and level of contribution which will be allowed into your discussion.

4) "I find it hard to follow along. I can't always hear what others are saying in the front the class."
   Indeed student have to pay attention to what their peers are saying. It is important that the professor finds a way to make the class clear and understandable to all. In the following

chapter we will discuss how to make students' comments relevant and heard.

5) "My classmates can be so rude."
As an instructor you have to maintain the classroom culture. It is up to you to set the tone and ensure that you provide an environment that is safe and open to learning for your students.

The good news is that all of these complaints are easy enough to solve. It just takes a bit of foresight, preparation and emphasis on your part.

3P's of Case Teaching: Plan, Prepare, Perform

This book is organized into three sections to help you become a great case teacher. The first section deals with **planning** your course and your course materials. The emphasis of the planning section is to provide guidance on the choice of style, cases and materials for your class. This section centers around; "what is an appropriate approach to your class?" If you understand the student's capabilities, background and motivations, it will be much easier to properly pitch your class to the students.

The second section of this book deals with **preparing** for the teaching day. Here we want to offer advice for how to ensure that both the faculty and the students are prepared for a great day in the classroom. If only one party is prepared and the other is not, it often leads to an underwhelming time in the classroom and a missed opportunity to captivate the eager (and sometimes not so eager) minds. There are a number of simple tips that can equip you, as a faculty member, to be ready for a great delivery and to ensure that the students are properly prepared and in the "right frame of mind" for the classroom discussion.

The third section of this book is organized to help you to **perform** better in the classroom. Advice, strategies and tips from outstanding faculty and educational researchers are put forth to help case teachers improve their delivery. While teaching a case may look spontaneous and free flowing, solid planning and preparation are the key to orchestrating the classroom symphony. The performance section builds on the planning and preparation chapters to help you meet your classroom goals and unlock your potential in the classroom.

Box Story 1[4]

"Universities were founded in Western Europe in 1050 and lecturing has been the predominant form of teaching ever since," says biologist Scott Freeman of the University of Washington, Seattle. But many scholars have challenged the "sage on a stage" approach to teaching science, technology, engineering, and math (STEM) courses, arguing that engaging students with questions or group activities is more effective.

To weigh the evidence, Freeman and a group of colleagues analyzed 225 studies of undergraduate STEM teaching methods. The meta-analysis, published in the *Proceedings of the National Academy of Sciences*, concluded that teaching approaches that turned students into active participants rather than passive listeners **reduced failure rates and boosted scores on exams by almost one-half a standard deviation.** "The change in the failure rates is whopping," Freeman says.

(*Continued*)

---

[4] Taken directly from Bajak, A (2014). Lectures aren't just boring, they're Ineffective, too, study finds. www.science magazine. Org.

(Continued)

And the exam improvement — about 6% — could, for example, "bump [a student's] grades from a B– to a B."

"This is a really important article — the impression I get is that it's almost unethical to be lecturing if you have this data," says Eric Mazur, a physicist at Harvard University who has campaigned against stale lecturing techniques for 27 years and was not involved in the work. "It's good to see such a cohesive picture emerge from their meta-analysis — an abundance of proof that lecturing is outmoded, outdated, and inefficient."

Although there is no single definition of active learning approaches, they include asking students to answer questions by using handheld clickers, calling on individuals or groups randomly, or having students clarify concepts to each other and reach a consensus on an issue.

Freeman says he's started using such techniques even in large classes. "My introductory biology course has gotten up to 700 students," he says. "For the ultimate class session — I don't say lecture — I'm showing PowerPoint slides, but everything is a question and I use clickers and random calling. Somebody droning on for 15 minutes at a time and then doing cookbook labs isn't interesting." Freeman estimates that scaling up such active learning approaches could enable success for tens of thousands of students who might otherwise drop or fail STEM courses.

Chapter 2

PREPARING

Getting Started

Choosing a style: First of all, it is important to recognize that there is no "one right way" to teach a case. There are many styles that work and it is important that you choose a style that works for you and your class. Some people are able to demand long insightful comments and analysis by the students. Others run their class with many quick and to-the-point student answers. Personally, I keep it light but lively, opting for a safe environment for the students. On the other hand, some of the most effective teachers I have ever met create a classroom dynamic that feels like a shark tank pitch process.

The appropriate style is a matter of your personal preference, personal comfort and capability as well as the student's background, learning stage and course goals. Said differently, "find a style that works for you and fits with where the students are!"

The right style is, thus, in part dependent on the students, and whether this is a mandatory class that they must take, or an elective that they have chosen to opt into. In the former, students might feel trapped and a bit put-out, that a course they would not have chosen otherwise demands so much effort every day.

Alternatively, students often do enjoy the intense grilling on every comment, but this is more likely to be the case in elective classes. If the student self-selects into a class that offers an intense combative discussion format, then all is fair game. Thus, the style that is right may depend as much on the audience as it does on you.

Personally, I have taught both core and required courses. The self-selection bias of the audience is readily apparent. When I teach my electives, students know that I will be using cases and only those that want this experience choose to enter. Alternatively, when I am teaching a required or core class, the audience has great differences in their level of desire to participate each day. The length of questions and responses I give and get is quite different.

Knowing the Audience

We will discuss case teaching styles in greater detail, a bit later. We will offer advice on when and where some should be adopted. But for now, just recognize that you want to conduct your teaching in a manner that best suits you and delivers a quality experience for your class — and that there are many ways to do that.

Some simple considerations can help you to match your style to your audience. Keep in mind the age, the experience, the language competency, culture and the gender of your audience.

Age

The age of your audience and the teaching style you choose is an interactive formula. If you are relatively old compared to the students, you can scare them a bit. As most faculty age, they tend to soften in their teaching style. While some faculty report that they put up with less as they age, it is much more like the way they interact with their children. Realizing some battles are not worth fighting.

Additionally, older faculty tend to dress down, to reduce the age gap between the students and themselves. Conversely, young faculty often dress in power clothes and create a more exacting and demanding classroom environment as they struggle to establish their credibility. Young faculty who are teaching to executives often go too far in their attempt to establish credibility — only to find that what the executive audiences often want is a form of corporate therapy, rather than a dictator on the stage.

There is nothing we can do to change our age or the age of our students. But, what we do not want to do is to unnecessarily aggravate preconceived stereotypes. Being significantly older than the students and then delivering dated materials and cases to the class can provoke the refrain "this professor is out of touch" or worse yet, "the world has passed this professor by." If you are going to teach older material be sure you justify why it is there, reference what is happening today or will happen in the future, and if you can, show the students how this phenomenon has actually happened to many firms or managers throughout history. Older material is not to be avoided, no matter what your age is, as it is often a way of teaching and demonstrating robust and universal truths. Just be mindful that the audience is constantly judging you. Don't unknowingly become a part of a stereotype.

Gender

Throughout areas such as SE Asia and Western Asia, the higher education participation rate is greatly skewed toward females. For example, in Thailand, the female to male participation rate at the top schools is roughly 3 to 1. The applications at the graduate level are even more dramatically shifted toward females. Your gender mix within the classroom may call for a different tone. For instance, a male professor may not want to be too overbearing in a largely female classroom. Similarly, the manner in which questions are asked is very different. Numerous studies and my own experience indicate that men tend to be more competitive, have higher risk taking profiles and are less self-conscious than women. Direct confrontational questions may work like a charm with a heavily male audience, but not as well in a largely female audience.

I give below an example to demonstrate which style is more appropriate. Suppose the question can be framed in two ways. Question 1 states, "How can you possibly advocate this approach given fact A and fact B?", and Question 2 can be worded as, "Given that A and B are what they are, do you think there might be alternative answers?"

Q1 is a straight to the issue confrontation of the student. Much like a courtroom where the facts are put in front of the witness in an alternative format and you are asking them to re-answer outside of their comfort zone. This may work well for the combative nature of entrepreneurial males. Q2 is a much gentler way of asking students to reconsider. Which you choose may have a lot to do with your audience's gender, employment field or what you are preparing them for. The first question is ideally suited for entrepreneurs that will be pitching their ideas in a shark tank and struggling to gain support and funding to keep their firms alive. The second question is a gentler way to promote different logical analysis.

Experience

The younger and less experienced your class is, the less you can depend on the class for *correct insights* that will help the case move along efficiently. Instead, you may find yourself in the role of extending the students comments and providing mini-examples and lectures to supply the missing support that the students are not yet trained for or prepared to supply. With well-intentioned, but not yet trained and competent students, your role in the class has to be a bit different than when you are teaching executives or practitioners with decades of experience.

Experienced managers often want to discuss the intricacies of their problems and the difficulties that they are individually facing. This can be a dangerous path for the novice instructor to go down. If you let the experienced manager talk about their problems, they are going to expect solutions. Here the instructor needs to be able to say, "I won't have all the facts to answer a question like that, but let's see what some of the folks in the class think. Does anybody have a solution for (name)?" This allows the student to frame their problem and seek the wisdom of the class. On the other hand, most of the student problems can be answered by the examples you have prepared for your case. After you have taught a case once or twice, you start to see what the obvious questions are from the class. You should prepare an illuminating answer that is waiting for that question. This can raise the student's perception of the faculty as a true expert in their field. Such "seemingly spontaneous" answers go a long way in establishing credibility.

Language competency

How competent the audience is with the language of instruction changes many, many, many different parts of your teaching style! When the language of instruction is clearly a second language, you have to be prepared to accept shorter answers from your students. Also, your questions and your statements need to be shorter. Long passages are often harder for the second language students to comprehend the subject or question being asked.

Your questions need to be free from idiomatic expressions that don't directly translate. In your native language, relating with localized or hip terms and slang may bring you closer to your audience. But, in teaching abroad you may just find that you are confusing large segments of your class.

Culture

Obviously, different cultures have different norms. Depending on the culture you are conducting your workshop in, and where you are from, you have to adopt the style you think will suit you best. Teaching in North America, a direct and confronting style of questioning and drilling down on student answers will work well. People tend to be much more direct and confrontational as they take the approach that *"Iron sharpens Iron."* In Asia, however, the concept of "face" is very important. That is, Asian executives and students don't want to lose face (feel embarrassed) in front of their peers. Thus, you need to keep the questioning style a little lighter and less confrontational.

Also, your country of origin may carry with it deep stereotypes or cultural baggage. If your country has fought wars, colonized or had a diplomatic row with the government of the primary participants in your class, your tone should be much less confrontational than if you have been nation partners that are unified on numerous dimensions.

Current topics

Pay attention to the events of the world. While your theories may not change, how you are discussing topics may be important. Hotly contested elections, wars, terrorist events or current social topics can be potential flash points in the classroom. You need to make sure that, even if you can't avoid the land mines, you are aware that they are there.

Personal Insight: I remember teaching in Austria the week that the United States entered Iraq under George Bush. The war was extremely unpopular in Europe and being an American, I could feel the resistance and even resentment to every statement I made. After 30 minutes I stopped, explained my personal position on the events and asked for any final comments. Then I said, "Let's not have any of this stand in the way of what we have to talk about in this class." The class went very well after that. But the key was that I was aware that this might be a problem and I was prepared to address it if need be.

The more difficult situations are when you are not aware of the problem. You can be teaching and trying to get folks to discuss something but getting literally nowhere. I have found that it is a good idea to call an impromptu 5 minute Bio-break and pull some of the students aside and ask them if something is wrong. Perhaps they did not get the materials? Or, students did not receive the instructions for the case? Or, they were told something in conflict from the programme office? Or they just misread your syllabus? If any of these problems are happening, it is better to be aware and try to adjust on the fly if you can.

Choosing Cases

The starting point for case teaching is always the choice of case. Through the years, many young faculty and students have asked me "How do you choose the cases for your class?" There are several dimensions that you need to keep in mind but the following is a list I feel quite strongly about.

1) Choose cases that fit with your curriculum. Faculty often opt for cases about the most popular companies. While this is not a bad idea, as students generally show higher interest in companies they know about, you need to be certain that the case actually helps you to teach the topics that you need to teach. In the end, you are trying to develop competent young professionals. Your case is a pedagogical tool to assist you in that mission. Cases that do not help you to instruct what you want to teach will inevitably need to be replaced.

2) The best case is the case that helps you meet the learning objectives of that day. When you structure your course, you are generally breaking the entire learning journey down into a series of days and topics that must be taught. You want to be sure that the cases you choose fit not just your curriculum, but where you are in the course on that day. There are often very good and exciting cases that will engage the students and give everyone a wonderful experience, but they don't really help you to deliver your curriculum or build the foundational competencies that you will rely on later in the course.

   Where you are in the course often determines what you can teach in a case. If the students do not have the requisite understanding of certain material or the background and grounding to understand the concepts presented in the case at that time, much of the potential learning will be lost. Most courses are built on a series of theories that form the pillars for later topics and more integrative and comprehensive teaching. Cases that help you build those pillars when you need them are the best cases.

3) The best cases for you to teach "don't include the kitchen sink!" As we will talk about shortly, when you teach, you have a

limited period of time to teach the case at hand. Having very complex and multifaceted cases can present some not so obvious challenges.

a. Students must be of a certain level of competency and training in the degree programme to actually be able to understand concepts that are not being directly covered in *your* course. Thick and multidimensional cases are best used for capstone and corporate strategy classes where all of the elements of the firm might be coming under the scrutiny of the student. These courses are reserved for the end of the degree programme when students have had the exposure and experience with all of the dimensions of the firm.

b. Many times you can't teach a complex case in a single class period as there simply is not enough time. If you have a three or four-hour class period, you can use longer cases. But if it is an hour or 75 minutes class, you really need to choose cases with a limited number of topics that can be discussed properly.

c. Along with the challenge for the students to be able to participate and answer questions, *YOU the faculty,* must also be prepared to answer questions that might not be from your domain or might not fit with the course you are teaching. If you require the students to read the case and you are teaching marketing, and there are a host of operations, finance or logistics issues in the case, they are rightfully going to ask for your opinion and expertise on some of those issues. While there may be an opportunity for cross disciplinary integration, there are not many faculty who feel extremely comfortable teaching out of course and out of domain topics.

Summary: *So beware of the case that takes you into areas you don't want or don't feel comfortable teaching.*

4) The best cases are cases that allow you to be the expert. You want to teach cases that fit your curriculum as completely and directly as possible, but also where you can be far ahead of the class in your preparation and understanding. While you are never competing with your students, you do want to be seen as the person that carries around the final answers to the case, and that you are armed with more information than what the case has in it.

   So the best cases either have a great teaching note, or they are easy for you to research, or to find management parallels. If you have worked at the company in the case, or at a competitor, or just have deep experience in the industry, you will find that these types of cases help you to establish your expertise. Also, such cases are generally easier for you to understand and answer questions over, as you know the industry priorities and the challenges that managers face every day.

5) While it might sound a bit repetitive, find cases that have good teaching notes. While you will go beyond the teaching note to add your own personal insights and flair to the material, it helps to begin with a well thought out, well organized and detailed teaching note. The teaching note is most often crafted by the case-author as a guide to help you teach the case as they had intended it. Having taught the case themselves, the author should provide tips and insights into what has worked in the past and points that you need to be aware of.

   A good teaching note should first, provide you a sense of timing for how long each section of the case should take to teach. This is very useful in laying out your daily schedule for the class. You certainly don't want to use a case that takes three hours to teach, for a three-hour seminar, and then try to teach a host of additional topics. Second, the note should provide guiding questions for the case. These questions should be logically ordered for discussion, though you should always feel free to change the order to fit your methods of delivering the theories and learnings. Third, the best case notes give you an understanding of what theories can be applied to help answer each question and what specific calculations or insights the author believes are important. Additionally, a good case note will also provide an understanding of the questions and concerns that students might ask. And finally, a solid case note should provide an epilogue regarding what the company did, what they perhaps should have done, and what the results were.

You may also find that the length and depth of a teaching note can be very different from the case. In fact, a shorter case would probably have a lengthier teaching note, as it needs to provide more of the background and color to the case. As an example, perhaps one wants to look at Memaksa Steel (SMU-11-0001). The case is one page in length, but the teaching note is a full 8 pages.

6) The best cases can help you to listen and diagnose your class. Early in the semester it is a good idea to give open-ended cases that may not have correct answers but provokes opinion sharing. Such cases allow the students to express their opinions, views, and background knowledge. Listening to the way students discuss the material and the types of connections they make does a lot to help you understand their general competency level, orientation and perhaps cultural views. As you hear these, you can modify and pitch your lecture, case discussion and course accordingly.

As one travels around the world, there will be students with very different opinions and views about an open market, or the role of government, or the proper ethical standards and conduct of their society. Learning a bit about the baseline in an open and free discussion can help the instructor to present their course appropriately and avoid the "ugly foreigner" stereotype.

7) The best cases are those that are easy to teach and fit your style. Teaching styles can vary a bit. Some people are comfortable exploring the motives of the case actors, or then trying to gain insights into motivations and expected actions of the protagonist or their counterpart. Other instructors enjoy moving in a step-by-step manner through the analytical sections of a case, taking time to build on each analytic insight. Still, others may enjoy a case with a surprise ending or a climatic conclusion. Their preferred method is to build interest and deliver a solid conclusion. Whatever your style, find cases that fits it.

8) Make sure the case fits your class dynamics. The level of the students that you are teaching influences three decisions: 1) the length of the case, 2) the complexity of the case and 3) the depth of the case.

   a. Length: This is a tricky issue. Generally speaking, the undergraduate or polytechnic students need shorter cases, as they do not tend to prepare as well, and perhaps more importantly, they have less background to bring to the case. As an instructor teaching at this level, you realize your teaching goal is more about providing exposure to an industry or concepts and less geared toward practice and integration.

As you move toward graduate education, the students are expected to integrate concepts. Masters education is really about mastering the subject and the orientation is on integration synthesis and adaption of the material. By this level of study, students are often more diligent about preparing for the cases and they bring more experience to the process. The longest and most complex cases are generally used in graduate elective courses, where students have chosen to be in that course, and may soon be walking out the door to employ some of the concepts they have learned there. Much like the case teaching methods in hospitals or veterinary clinics, the student is expected to analyze, diagnose and recommend a course of action.

For executives taking a paid training course, the instructor may probably want to revert back to shorter cases. Executives have a tendency not to read, or if they have read, they do not do as deep a preparation as a Masters student might. This is partially due to a different student teacher contract. Degree seeking students realize that their course grade hangs in the balance with their classroom performance. If your case does not go perfectly one day, you can reprimand the students on their preparation and there is time for them to amend and learn "the rules of your road." On the other hand, for executives training, they will be filling out a single day's evaluation form of your course. If it does not go well, it can be a tough day.

Personal insight: You may choose longer cases when teaching executives, if the course is being monitored by their employers, or this is a highly visible and expensive programme either locally, or in the firm. I have had the opportunity to teach in several programmes that are attended by a small network of the nation's elite. In this sort of environment, the opinion of others is quite important and preparation can be high. But, in general, executives tend not to

*read fully. Therefore, I like to be able to stop and give them 15 min-
utes to read the case again if I find that the preparation level is low.
The worst teaching days come when you assign a 25-page case and
no one has read it. But if you assign a 4-page case and no one has
prepared, you can take 15 minutes out and level set the class.*

b. Complexity: With age, training, and seniority comes
   greater opportunity for complex cases. 18-year-old Polytechnic students may not have the background, exposure
   or skills to handle complex multifaceted case. Alternatively,
   senior executives may not be content with cases that view
   the problem from a single lens. They may be sitting in an
   operations class, or a marketing seminar, but they come
   with very well thought out and highly developed experiences and mindsets that cause them to ask: *"What does
   this mean for me?"* Restated differently, executives are
   not only competent to handle complex cases — they often
   demand it.

c. Much like complexity, the more senior the audience is, the
   greater level of depth they can handle. In an undergraduate
   classroom you may want to make students aware of what
   a sales force is, what it does, and why it is important. At
   the graduate level, you may want the students to understand that a sales force is an important resource, it can be
   managed in a number of ways and the following are theories that can be applied to this. In working with executives,
   they are often very focused on how to turn these theoretical propositions into management activities that can affect
   their performance. They spend much of their time not just
   learning the concept and understanding its importance, but
   thinking about how to use it to enhance firm performance.
   They often want the theory, the guide for implementing

that theory, the metrics for monitoring and insuring performance, and potential means by which it can be adapted and better adopted.

9) The best cases are interesting, fascinating, relevant and or illuminating. While it seems easy to say this, it is a bit harder in practice. Guessing what students or executive participants might find important may not be so straight forward, but a few simple principles to keep in mind can help.

   a. Choose cases that are regionally relevant to the students or the topics. Continuously using North American cases in an Asian or South American classroom is a common source of complaints on student evaluation forms. Students in less developed environments often can't see the opportunity for applying the lessons of the cases that they study from the developed markets. The macro environmental context is often so different that they struggle with understanding the relevance of the case. So, if you must use the highly developed Western cases, be prepared to demonstrate or show students how these can be adapted or applied in their local environments.

   b. Finding cases that are from their industry, a parallel industry or an exciting industry often helps mature students to be more interested in the topic. While you may not want to teach a semi-conductor product development case to a group of semi-conductor engineers, a case about product development in pharmaceuticals or medical device technology might be a relatively similar industry structure with similar product development cycles, etc. Some industries can be compared very easily (e.g., hotels and hospitals which are both very asset intensive, property bound, selling rooms which expire each day) while other industries are not (e.g., hospitals and agriculture).

c. Products or services that are relevant are always more interesting than products that the students would never see. A battle of two micro beers in the United States would have virtually no interest to a Filipino student. But talk to them about two local craft beers and you might find more interest. Again, if you want to talk about two regional players in the states, say coffee chains such as Caribou Coffee and Seattle's Best, be prepared to talk about the local chains where you are teaching.

d. Finding things that people never thought of is a good way to fascinate them. One of the highest selling cases of all time is Harvard's Optical Distortions Inc., which is about the viability of a business concept of making red contact lenses for chickens. The lenses obscure the chicken's vision and reduce their cannibalistic tendencies leading to higher egg yields. Students are often fascinated with what they never imagined was possible.

10) When in doubt, look at what others are teaching and find cases that have a unique place. While you never want to teach only what others leave you, you also want to be sure that you are not treading the same ground or not teaching the same cases. Cases that fit, not with just your course, but with the degree programme objectives of your institution or client are always preferred. Just as "no man is an island", no class or case session is completely divorced from your institution, programme or degree. You want to be certain that the cases you will teach are not being taught by other instructors at your institution. This can present great challenges for you if the students have already discussed the case.

Box Story 2: The Problem with Popular Cases: And How to Handle Them

When you opt for popular cases you have to be aware of four potential problems.

1) The same cases that you find popular may also be taught in other classes as other instructors may also find these companies and their problems interesting. One of the worst teaching experiences you can have is when the students have had the same case in a previous class. Moreover, when they begin telling you that according to one of your colleagues the answers are different. Having already heard a discussion on the case, some students may be far ahead of their peers and that frustrates other members of the class. Their frustration will most probably be aimed at the faculty for poor course planning, rather than their peers.

   Also, having had the case earlier, the students may rush to the solutions too quickly for your liking. Part of the art of teaching a case is to think through how you want the student to digest the material. Much like a movie script, you want to be delivering the material in chunks and bites, saving some solutions and insights for your climatic ending. But when they are armed with the insights and answers from another class, you have to watch out that they do not blurt out solutions that you intend to save for your climax.

2) With popular cases you may find that the students can pose problems for your delivery. For one, it could be that the students have greater experience with the company,

(*Continued*)

(*Continued*)

brand, or product than you do. This sort of expertise can put you on the back foot. I remember teaching a class of EMBAs, where the student, unbeknownst to me, had actually been the protagonist of the case. In this sort of situation your facilitation skills become paramount to your survival. Instead of being the ultimate expert, you might find yourself teasing out insights from the class expert.

The second problem with student experience may have to do with what the students know. They may be knowledgeable, but not on the topic you are trying to teach. Weaponized with their own personal experiences and insights, they might continuously take you to topics that are personally relevant, but not what you want to be teaching. Frankly, when students scan the syllabus and see familiar names, they often think that will be one of the days "I am going to shine in the classroom as I know so much about this company." Trying to harness and discourage that can be problematic.

3) Popular cases may be used at your school as well as other schools around the globe. The more popular the case is, the more likely that there are case notes and solutions readily available on the web or at your school. These sort of materials defeat much of the benefit of the case teaching method. Students do not have to sift through an avalanche of data trying to string together logical arguments that sum into a decision. Instead, they simply recite the answers as laid out.

(*Continued*)

(Continued)

4) Popular cases become worn very quickly. Very often, all of the faculty are, at the very least, talking about the company in their class, even if they do not give the formal case study. Depending on when you were in school you heard about the news-makers of that day and time. While it might be good to hear about the financial impact of Google's decisions, or their HR policies, or their data mining of big data or their innovation strategies...the students can get bored. While there is always an argument that we should have cases that take an integrated look at a company, students eventually want to hear about something else.

Chapter 3

STUDENT PREPARATION

Student Preparation

As you think about the classroom experience, you need to consider that this is a symphony to be performed between you and the students. Both parties have a very important part to play, and both must be prepared to deliver the music that is on the sheets that day. In this chapter, we will explore a number of steps that you can take to ensure that students are ready and well prepared for the classroom. Then, we will provide a number of suggestions for helping you, the instructor, to prepare for the classroom.

Supporting Student Preparation

In contrast to faculty-centered lectures, the case method is truly a student-centered learning pedagogy. Thus, unlike lectures, you are only in control of a part of the process. To have a great class discussion you need the students to be prepared that day! Unlike lectures, where the student may be able to read after the class-period and gain a grasp of the course concepts, they must be prepared for the case the day it is taught to them and their peers to get the full benefit of the case process. To get the deep peer-to-peer participation, students must be fully prepared for the class. To aid student preparation, it is helpful to understand that you need to ensure that there is:

A) A standard level of preparation for the pedagogy and
B) Activities that help the student be prepared for that specific lecture.

A) Preparing for the cases: Getting the students prepared for the pedagogy

Case teaching is not like lecturing. Students must be prepared and they must be prepared in the right way for a classroom experience to reach it's potential. So how do we get students to come to class in the *"right"* frame of mind for case discussions? To do this, you need to inform the students as to what are the rules of the road if you will. Their participation, learning, performance and satisfaction can all be improved by following these seven administrative steps early in the term.

1) Benefits and Penalties: The first step in getting students to adhere to a high daily standard of preparation is to inform them about the benefits of being prepared and the penalties for not being prepared. As a faculty, you need to think about how demanding and how steep you want each of these to be. Below are two paraphrased examples from actual syllabus of professors.

   a. "During the semester you will be, at least once, called upon to open a case (begin the case discussion) or be asked to rebut or add to the opening comments of your classmate. If you have not read the case and are thus unable to comment on the case or extend the opening remarks you will receive a one-letter grade reduction for the course. Thus, you will not be able to make a grade above B+ regardless of your exam scores or your other class participation scores."

b. "Each day you will receive a score for your class participation. You may earn up to three points in each class for your comments based on their quality and their volume. However, if you are called upon and unable to answer questions you will lose one point. Additionally if you do not come to class, you will receive a score of −2 for that day."

The first example is a very punitive policy towards poor class participation. I have seen this sort of grading policy in late stage, elective classes of a programme. The thought behind this is that each day that we discuss a case should be treated as an examination and your failure to prepare or answer is treated harshly. This method tends to be most often used in elective courses for a few reasons. Usually, as an elective, the students are aware of the faculty member's course requirements and they are not obligated to select the course. Students that enjoy a demanding high-risk classroom opt for such an experience. Also, there are many students that don't enjoy speaking in class. Instructors that wish to cull out the nonparticipating students will raise the stake for non-performance. This insures a rather committed, capable and engaged audience. It certainly makes the resulting class better prepared and creates a self-selected group of enthusiasts.

However, not all of our courses are electives, and not all of our students want to participate in a high stakes environment. Many foreign students come from cultures wherein speaking up in class is not seen as a socially positive trait. Additionally, their own comfort with the language of instruction may limit their ability to contribute to the discourse. Imposing very strict and punitive class discussion rules on these students may serve to be stressful and even counterproductive. Not to mention, when students become frustrated by the perceived injustice of such requirements, they often tend to hold it against the instructor.

2) Demonstrate What Is or Is Not an Acceptable Class Participation Point.

   In the early stages of your course, it is a good idea to tell students what is and is not acceptable or "grade-able" class participation. Be sure that students understand the actual demands and outcomes required in the class. This is one of the hardest things to explain as an instructor. Here you may want to clarify that participation is not just raising your hand and agreeing with the last comment, but adding to the logic, argument or discussion in a meaningful way.

   Also, you may want to establish with the students that you can only grade output in class. Students have a tendency to follow along, nod affirmatively, or even give a thumbs-up sign now and then. While it shows that they are paying attention, unfortunately it is hard to score as effective class contributions. When I asked one of the great teachers and case writers of all time (Ben Shapiro) how he graded class participation, he said, "Students often come to my office to complain about their class participation scores claiming I was prepared and I was paying attention. And I tell them that unfortunately, I can't grade input, I have to grade output. If you are not talking or contributing to the discussion, I have nothing to grade."

   You might look at "YouTube Zerrillo class participation video" for an instructive, though humorous tongue and cheek example of what is and is not class participation. It has been used in many classrooms worldwide.

   Early in the semester, it is a good idea to make specific references to outstanding examples of class participation. This helps the students to understand what is expected and what is exemplary. Similarly, pausing and focusing on improving a student's answer, or discouraging answers that subtract from the discussion, can be useful in setting standards for acceptable class comments.

3) Explain and Justify Your Grading Scheme and How Case Discussion Fits in:
As we discussed above, the students need to understand the rewards and penalties that occur in class every day. Make sure that they understand that grading class participation is not a simple "fudge factor" that is applied to round up or down the final grades. Be explicit and clear about how it will be graded. While I have used numerous scoring systems through the years, my own syllabus often reads as follows:

Students can score between –1 and 3 points in any class day. If you come to class and are not able to open or contribute to the discussion, you will lose 1 point for that day. If you do not come to class, you will lose 1 point for the day. If you come to class and do not say anything and do not contribute, you will score 1 point for the day[5]. Should you contribute several on point comments that demonstrate your preparation and insights you can score up to four points for the day. At the end of the semester, all of the student's points are totalled and they are ranked in the class from top to bottom.

Young instructors often ask at this point. How do you know how many points each student deserved for the day? There are many ways to grade class participation:

a. When you complete class each day, return to your office and record the daily scores. If you are teaching back-to-back

---

[5] Note: the punishment for no preparation should not be greater than the punishment for not attending class. If it is, students that have not prepared will not come to class. Even though they will not contribute to the discussion, you need them to progress in their thinking. Not attending is not helpful in their development.

classes, try to do it between classes. Your memory of the smaller comments offered in class will only decay with time. This can lead to student dissatisfaction with your scores.

b. You can record scores on your daily face sheet as you receive comments. However this ticking the student roster after some comments and possibly not others can lead to class distractions and anxiety. At times, you may find it useful to make a note of a particularly good comment if you are afraid you will not record it for some reason.

c. Assign a Teaching Assistant (TA) to record the scores while you are teaching. But if you are using a teaching assistant, it is a good idea to explain how you are assigning grades — that is, what a good comment is and is not. Also, be sure to run through the scores right after class to clear discrepancies and improve the TA's understanding of your standards.

d. One of the most innovative class participation recording policies was provided to me while I was running a case teaching seminar at a polytechnic college. The instructor has each student put a nameplate on their desk. On the back of the nameplate is a series of boxes corresponding to the class meeting date. At the end of the day the student is to mark what score they think they deserve for the day on (in this professor's scaling) a 3-point basis. The instructor would assign scores independently, and then compare his score to the self-assessed score the student assigned at the end of the day's class. He found that there was very little variance between scores and that students had a tendency to better estimate their class performance during the semester.

4) Explain to Students What They are *NOT* to do:
   In preparing for a case discussion, it is important that students do not search out past year's notes. Having the answers to the case before the discussion reduces the students learning opportunity and personal discovery. This short cutting of their analysis reduces the students synthesizing of data and formulation of their own arguments. Be they right or wrong, when the students develop their own solutions, they are more committed and engaged in the class discussion and analysis. Having answers before reading the case or engaging in a classroom discussion does not promote the deep and robust learning that comes with the twists and turns of a classroom drama.

   (Note: as an instructor, it should be mentioned that you probably do not want your case summary slides, should you produce them, to be handed out. If you let your solutions walk out of the classroom it is hard to ensure that future students do not have access to them. Also, you should warn that students should not access solutions to cases from the Internet.)

5) Tell the Student Why Participation is so Important for their Learning and That of their Classmates:
   Students will learn from their books, they will learn from the faculty and they will learn from each other. If they do not share their insights, they are robbing each other of the opportunity to learn. Explain to the students that both good and bad comments from your peers provide insights into the material, and shows how complex it is to others or how well their peers understand the material. These types of insights are important for leaders to recognize. Good leaders and good communicators know when it may be necessary to explain some of the more confusing points to their teams. Interacting with, watching and listening to your peers is a great step to being a leader and a great communicator.

6) Have Regular Intervals to Discuss How the Student is Performing on Class Participation:

   In tip 4, we discussed the need to record class participation. It is a good idea to offer the students the opportunity to periodically assess their performance. Periodic reviews reduce end of semester surprises and they provide you an opportunity to counsel the student on how to be a better or more regular contributor.

7) Provide a Preparation Template for How They Should Generally Prepare for a Case.

   There are a number of ways to guide the student's preparation. You might ask them to skim the case first to become aware of the major issues in the case. Ask them to concentrate on the major problem at hand and the solution being requested. Then begin to analyze the facts and look to your course work for theories that might help you better analyze and develop an integrated solution for the company issue. Just how you want them to prepare often depends on the students' level of competency and their experience with the domain. That is, students with limited backgrounds and limited classroom experience may not be able to pull together integrated solutions. (But then, you probably should not be using multifunctional complex cases with this level of student.) The following are examples taken from syllabi that help students to prepare for class discussions or in writing a case.

   Preparing a case for class discussion. In preparing an analysis, read through the case looking for the main problems that you need to address. Develop a rationale for your belief that the problems identified are in fact problems. In addition, after a closer reading, assemble the factual information presented in the case that addresses various problems.

Once you have assembled all the information provided, develop a framework for analysis. This framework should (1) identify problem areas, (2) provide evidence that indicates why the problem is indeed a problem and the alternative ways in which it may be resolved, and (3) choose a course of action that you feel is based on the soundest assumptions. By following this strategy, you will be able to develop an integrated analysis and will avoid focusing on issues for which there is little data.

Writing up a Case

If you are going to give a case as a written assignment, it is a good idea to provide them with a writing format. A standardized format helps you to more easily assess the students' works against that of their peers. As an example, I use the following headings:

1. Purpose of the Report: State the purpose of the report. Specify the problems to be addressed in your analysis.

2. Recommendations: State the manner in which each of the problems you have identified should be resolved. In this section, only your recommendations should be given. Reasons for the recommendations should appear in the analysis.

3. Analysis: This is the heart of your report. It entails marshaling factual data that supports your problem identification and your recommended course of action. In essence, it is the linkup between problem and recommendations.

   For example, if the first issue you address in your analysis is the target audience, use target audience as a side heading. If the next issue is creative strategy, use it as a side heading.

4. <u>Summary:</u> The summary is a brief recap of the problem statement, your recommendation and the logic that you supplied during the analysis section. This is your opportunity to restate what you believe the problem is, the course of action you recommend and emphasize the logic you employed.

Common Errors in Case Writing

1. Format outlined above is not followed. Subheadings are not used in the analysis section.

2. Problem and Recommendation sections are too long. No more than half a page is generally needed for each of these sections. Use outline form and dot points throughout the written report. There is no need for complete prose. However, do not use shorthand that is unintelligible, even to you at some later point in time.

3. Focus centers on minor issues or issues for which there is little or no data. Let the case facts guide you to the selection of issues. If there is little or no data addressing an issue, don't dwell on it in your analysis.

4. Rehashing of case data. Assume the reader is familiar with the case. Present case data <u>only</u> when it is needed to support a line of reasoning you are developing. Don't summarize the case situation as a preamble to your analysis, and don't present case facts unless you are going to drive home a point with them. You can assume that the reader/instructor is the CEO or at least a member of the management team. Thus, it is not important to write long prose speaking about the history of the firm and the background of the protagonist etc.

5. Non-critical evaluation of case data. Before you use evidence presented in the case, ask yourself if it was collected in a sound

manner and whether it is relevant to the issue that you are addressing. This does not give you a license to eliminate all data. Rather, you want to qualify the conclusions you reach by evaluating the quality of the data on which a conclusion is based. Often times, cases will have a simple observation by a sole member of the management team, and this is being used factually within the firm. However, as a counter to this opinion, overwhelming statistical observations and evidence may have been collected. It is important that you weigh the evidence that you are using.

6. A failing to provide a rationale for eliminating the alternatives you have not chosen. It is important to show that the recommended course of action is likely to deal effectively with the problems identified. It is equally important to provide a rationale for dismissing un-chosen alternative courses of action.

7. Failure to present analytical work in an understandable manner. When performing computations, be sure your presentation (usually in an appendix) is sufficiently detailed so the reader/ instructor can replicate the analysis. This requires you to indicate where the data came from and show how it is analyzed. Thus it is a good idea to footnote or cite where in the case certain facts came from and the calculations you performed to arrive at your point/conclusion.

In summary, these seven tips can help you to establish the administrative ground rules for your class. Letting the students know what is a good answer, how they will be graded, the need for preparation and the penalties for a failure to prepare, how their grades will be determined, and how they should or should not prepare will go a long way in ensuring that the students are knowledgeable about what is expected. If they do not comply with the ground rules as spelled out, it is probably not from ignorance but rather a lack of effort. As an instructor, your obligation is to provide the opportunity for students to engage, and informing them of what is expected and what is to be done is a crucial first step.

B) Preparing the students for TODAY'S class:

While the general level of commitment and engagement by the students can be raised by following the seven steps above, each day and each case is different and it requires different preparation. Getting the students to properly prepare for the upcoming class is yet another challenge of case teaching that must be met. The good news is that this is in some ways easier than getting them to comply with the rules of the road. Five easy tips to help are as follows:

1) What Questions Might be Important in Getting the Students Prepared for Today's Case?
   This is your first step in guiding your case discussion and lecture! As you think about the case discussion and how you want the discussion to flow, you need to think about what questions you will ask and what questions you want the students to be prepared to answer. In graduate electives, instructors often do not supply questions to the case, as part of the pedagogy is to have the students identify the issues and challenges of the case. Alternatively, for more junior students, providing questions helps to insure that the preparation is correct. Over time, students have come to expect, or more directly demand, questions to help their preparation. If you chose not to provide them, you may want to think about offering a reason why you are not, as students may interpret this as you being out of touch with their needs or just not concerned with their learning.

2) What Supplemental Materials Will Help Students to Prepare?
   Case analysis is an extraordinary way to introduce theories and frameworks to the students and demonstrate the managerial usefulness and integration of such. Often times, you may want the students to read a theory or framework prior to

attempting a case. When the students have read the theories or frameworks and then try to apply them, they are more likely to understand the concepts in broader detail. Moreover, they move beyond memorizing and recalling a concept to the higher order process of employing that concept in analyzing and problem solving.

Cases are also a great means to teach students about industries, cultures, laws, economies or regions. Sometimes, parts of the case will be better understood with more background materials. Students in developed economies, with explicit laws and years of stability, often can't grasp some of the nuances that strangle commerce in developing markets (the reverse might be true for students from developing countries), and providing supplemental materials on the region or the macro environment is often useful in helping the student to better understand the context in which the case is occurring.

Having greater background also helps the student to better read the case, Part of our interpretation of any passage of prose has to do with our past learnings and what we are aware of. The more aware the students are of the area, problems, and challenges, the more insightful and better-developed solutions we see. Obviously there needs to be a balance here, as you do not want to assign copious amounts of background readings just to ensure the student has background, as they may lose focus on the primary topic to be covered (the case).

3) What Role Do You Want The Students to Prepare For?
Sometimes you may want to have one group of students play the part of the firm's management, while another group of students take on the role of competitor. Such role-playing can help the students to understand the dynamic nature of their solutions and how competitive reactions may limit their strategic bounds.

Other options might be that different groups of students assume different functional roles. Say one group is from strategy, another from operations and a third from finance or marketing. By having students take different functional roles for the same case, it forces them to view their solutions from different lenses. Or, it might be useful to have students take the roles of different stakeholders such as patients, doctors, family caregivers and payers. These types of role-plays can help students understand the breadth of answers possible and how they might craft solutions that better serve a wide range of constituencies/stakeholders.

4) Should Students Seek Information From Someone?
   Having the students ask questions of buyers, users, or regulators of a good or service, or their own managers or subordinates, can help them to come to class with real life data and stories to share. Numerous studies indicate that when they have collected specific data, students are more willing to participate in the classroom as they want to share that data. While such exercises help students to become more aware of a problem and make the case more relevant, you need to watch out! Students often come to class wanting to tell you what is the right answer that they got from the horse's mouth. When their sources are role models or held in high esteem, your refuting their expert's points may not sit well. Telling a student, in front of their peers, that their father or mother may have handled the management situation wrongly is a delicate needle to thread.

5) Should Different People or Groups Answer Different Parts of the Case or Different Questions?
   In longer cases, or when you have limited time to teach, it is important to have a group of people fully prepared to answer the questions you need answered. With long cases in large

classes students often risk that they will not be called on and they don't prepare deeply for the case. By assigning a limited number of questions to particular students and or groups ahead of class, you are notifying them that they will be expected to answer these questions. Knowing what they will have to answer, they tend to prepare more fully.

This selective preparation reduces the potential for those awkward moments when the students are not prepared and have to admit it in class. Or worse yet, the students provide a wholly incorrect or ill prepared answer which derails a case discussion that is narrowing to a climax.

Similarly, you may want to tell a student ahead of time that they will be expected to do something or prepare something special for class. When a student has had a poor performance in class, you may say, "Next class, Linda will get the chance to redeem herself by opening the case." This sort of advance notice is a good tactic for assisting shy students to be prepared and able to answer the opening question.

Summary: Student preparation for the day, much like setting the ground rules, requires the faculty to guide the students' activities to ensure that they are ready to answer the right questions. In general, the more prepared the students are, the easier it is to get them to engage and enlighten their peers. Student participation and preparation can be highly variable depending upon the culture, institution or programme that you are teaching in. Leaving it to chance can lead to some very difficult experiences. Following the 12 steps set aside in this chapter can go a long way toward reducing that variability and towards providing a great platform for learning.

Box Story 3

In the late 1990's and early 2000's, I was the Associate Dean of the Graduate Programme at the University of Texas' McCombs School of Business. BusinessWeek reported the school to be the number 2 MBA programme in the world for entrepreneurship. The entrepreneurship programme was focused on starting, managing and harvesting ventures. All of the faculty were very highly rated by the students and heavily invested in case teaching. The school often brought in outside faculty to conduct case teaching seminars for the faculty. Working hard to hone their craft, they demanded much from their students in terms of classroom preparation and they gave as they got. It was a fantastic experience for the students that took the courses.

During the 1990's, Thailand would routinely be reported to be among the most entrepreneurial nations in the world with the highest levels of per capita entrepreneurs. While many of these were small Mom & Pop style business ventures, the Thai college graduates were among the most likely to start businesses as opposed to joining corporations. Teaching concurrently at that time in Thailand at Thammasat University, I was not surprised by these statistics as many of my domestic Thai students followed this path.

Over a two-year period, we admitted 13 Thai students to the University of Texas MBA. Given my teaching responsibilities in Thailand, I personally interviewed each of the 13 students. Twelve of them wanted to come to the University of Texas to

(Continued)

(Continued)

study entrepreneurship (the other, marketing). Over the ensuing two years, I tracked their progress and stayed in touch with them as their Dean, and as someone that felt responsible for them as they went to school far from home. As they were graduating, I sat down with each student to talk about their journey and get their insights. What I found was that none of the students had actually pursued the entrepreneurship track at Texas. As I spoke to them, most of them said that they "did not feel comfortable in a course with a high percentage of the grade based on class discussion." Instead, they opted for courses where exams were a higher percentage of their final score. In the end, seven of the students opted into the finance track.

Chapter 4

FACULTY PREPARATION

Case teaching, while rewarding, is tough! Unlike lectures, you are only in control of part of the process. You also need attentive, willing, prepared and engaged students to bring a case to life. While we have spoken at length about how to support the student prepare for the case discussion, it is important to recognize that you, the faculty, must also be prepared for the class interaction that will soon take place. Your preparation can go a long way in determining how the class flows, the reception of key learning point, student morale, and engagement.

For first time teachers moving away from instructor-centered teaching to student centered learning, the adoption of cases is like throwing away the crutches and trying to run. The customized, somewhat idiosyncratic learning journey requires at times an orchestra conductor and at other times a bit of a train engineer. At times, you are building pace, passion, and excitement; and at other times, you are making sure that all arrive at the intended passenger destinations... on time!

Case discussions require you to ask questions. And, asking questions can take you anywhere. This is especially true, if you have not thought about where you want to go with your class discussion. Like a symphony, all of the musicians in the hall need to be playing from the same sheet of music. But, like a train conductor, we will not arrive on time if we don't keep on time and stay on the tracks. Below we introduce ten steps to help successfully plan your lecture.

There are a number of issues you should consider as you think about your upcoming case discussion and how you want the discussion to flow.

1) Understand what the case is needed for?
   As you choose a case and deliver it, you need to understand why you are using this case. Is it to develop deep analytical skills with the topic at hand? Or are you just trying to start a classroom conversation as a means to demonstrate the relevance of a topic area? Is this a case that integrates with other frameworks, or a separate theory meant to be taught as a standalone concept?

2) How long should the case last?
   Depending on how long your classes are or where you are in your course, you want to be aware of how much time you can actually dedicate to this case. If you don't have a general idea of how long you want the case to last, you can get into awkward situations in which you finish class too early, or are hopelessly late and rushing to teach other concepts which might require greater time.

3) What is my opening question?
   Starting the case discussion is an important step. Determining what your first question will be and who will be receiving it has a lot to do with striking the tone of the discussion and guiding your class forward. How broad, or how focused, your first question is often determines the types of answers and discussion that you get.

What is going on in this case? This is a broad and open question that invites students to tell you the background factors of the case under study. Asking, *"What should this company have done?"* calls for a very different set of responses that are much more solution oriented. How much time you have and what you are trying to accomplish may change the questions you want to ask.

4) How will I use the instructional technologies that are available?
   As you think about student learning, you have to be aware that the students pay great attention to what is on the board or shown on the classroom monitors. Planning how you will display key issues, analysis, summarization or future-learnings can aide greatly in the student's absorption of the course concepts and materials. Your board and alternate technologies have a lot to do with what is retained, understood, and remembered.

5) What summary points will I make?
   Great case discussions generally have great summaries. As you go through the effort of building a classroom discussion, you need to consider how you are going to end it. Much like a stage play, the students want to hear the summary of what they should have learned, why this was important, and what should they now be able to do.

6) What future (past) points or course concepts will this discussion help me make?
   As an instructor you realize that the case is often part of a semester, or programme's long journey. As you consider the case you are teaching, you want to think about how it integrates with, exemplifies, or sets up future (or past) learning points. Students enjoy seeing that the concepts they have studied are robust enough to have been used in multiple cases or settings.

7) In what order will I raise the points that are central to the case? There will be numerous learning points in a case. Which one you want to address first, second, third etc., is often dependent on your style, your course goals and the best way to build the case drama and excitement. Keep in mind, you are in control of the ordering of the topics to be addressed and the emphasis you will put on each.

8) What *Can I,* or *Should I,* disclose?
Your case is your intellectual material. You need to think about what points or information you are willing to disclose, and In what manner. As mentioned above, letting your complete solutions walk out of the classroom can reduce the prep done by future generations of students. Additionally, if you are the case author and you have additional details on the company or individuals being discussed, you need to recognize what you are authorized to disclose.

9) How much should I listen? And how much should I talk?
Where you are in your course and what you are trying to accomplish with the case may change your role in the discussion. For instance, when you are assigning cases early in the semester, you may want to listen to the students a bit more as you want to diagnose their general understanding of the materials or the area of study. On the other hand, cases that are in the heart of the course that require new calculations and new skills to be taught may require that you, the instructor, supply small summaries or mini lectures to elaborate on the concepts and materials as the discussions are going forward.

10) Keep a file
Teaching a case is an evolving process. You will constantly be coming across information about the company and/or the industry it is in, and each time you teach, you will encounter

novel questions and gain new insights. Keeping a growing teaching file is a key step in preparing better for the future.

Getting Prepared

Step 1) **What will this case help me to do?** The first step in teaching a case is to ask and answer a few short questions such as: Where are you in the course you are teaching? Why is this case important to the course? What will this case do to help your teaching goals? For those teaching executive education or professional programmes, this particular class day may be a stand-alone single interaction that you will have with the students, or it may be part of a short programme, a term, a certificate, or even a diploma. How often will you interact with the students, the learning expectations and the course objectives has a lot to do with what you might try to accomplish with your case. Here are just a few examples:

a) **To set the learning objectives and provide emphasis:** One thing you never want to underestimate is the power of your pulpit as an instructor. Your choice of cases and what to emphasize in the cases has a lot to do with your ability to communicate the learning goals of your teaching to the students. Your own passion and interest for the material can enhance the curiosity and participation of the students. Having a solid first case in a semester or programme, that allows you to demonstrate your passion and your emphasis for certain topic areas, can go a long way in establishing the class culture, discussion style and your relationship with the audience.

b) **Diagnosis:** Sometimes, we have case discussions designed to understand the level of understanding of the students. If I am teaching students for an entire term, I would like to, early on, get an understanding of what they know and what they don't know. When you are new to a university or a corporate client, it is good to have a broad low risk case that allows for a lot of opinions to be offered during discussion. As the students give their opinions and provide support for their points, you generally come to know what frameworks they might have had in other courses, what cultural stereotypes they might hold, what things they really have no grasp of, or what motivates them. These insights can be very valuable as you move through the semester, as you can better link your material to the student's areas of interest or self-expressed gaps.

As an example, teaching Executive MBA's with 10 to 30 years of experience is a very diverse group. Some have been practicing business since they left university. Others are scientists, artists, public officials etc. It is good to provide a simple case or statement early in the semester and ask the students to respond. While there may be not right or wrong answers, you get the opportunity to understand what people think of when they think of the basic subject. (See Box Story).

c) **Introduction of new material:** A case study is often a way to bring new material to your class and have them understand the importance and relevance of the material. When teaching Human Resource Management or leadership, it is often useful to construct a scenario that puts the case actors in a difficult decision. The more that students can identify with the situation or their own potential probability of facing such a situation, the more interested they are in the topic. Regardless of the objective value of your course material, the students will not be likely to invest in learning it deeply if they do not understand its connection to their goals, motivations, desires or interest.

According to work at Carnegie Mellon University (see, for example, the Eberley Center for Teaching Excellence and Teaching Innovation),[6] demonstrating relevance to the student's academic lives, professional lives and personal interest can enhance student motivation to learn the topic. Connecting your material or case to real life enhances relevance. It also allows the student to understand how their learning such materials may make them more prepared for what lies beyond the classroom.[7]

Similar to using a case for the introduction of new material, you may also look at the case as a way to get the class talking about a topic. This can provide an excellent opportunity to bridge into a lecture on that topic. For instance, discussing moral dilemmas, crimes and punishments is often a great way to discuss the creation or application of laws or to demonstrate potential decision trees that may be more productive. Such examples work effectively as a lecture starter. In summary, person A facing situation Z and having to make a decision is a provocative way to engage a group's interest in the topic. Making the situation easy to understand, relevant and conceivable greatly enhances the probability that the topic cuts through the noise of the student's day and stimulates them to engage.

d) **To demonstrate and enhance application skills:** Sometimes, the case is used to introduce new materials. Other times the case is an opportunity to apply the skills and theories that the students have been acquiring throughout the course.

---

[6] https://www.cmu.edu/teaching/solveproblem/strat-lackmotivation/lackmotivation-01.html.

[7] http://archive.brookespublishing.com/articles/ed-article-0212.htm#reallife.

The case is an excellent vehicle to engage cognitive problem solving skills and apply analytic tools.

Just because a case calls for analytical or computational skills does not mean it has to be overly challenging. Simple single calculations early in the course can help students gain familiarity with calculations or tools and develop foundational competencies that you might call on later. Allowing students the opportunity to apply their newly found theories to moderately challenging material can promote their sense of accomplishment and confidence.

For people new to a domain or concerned about their competency, limited computational components can have a dramatic impact on their confidence and course assessment. It is no secret that courses such as Accounting and Finance routinely receive higher core course evaluations than Marketing or Human Resources at the full-time MBA level. Younger students want to feel as though they have skills that will help them to stand apart and be professional. Calculations provide an opportunity to develop and demonstrate mastery of a tool. As the tool box grows, so does the students appreciation and sense of accomplishment.

e) **Will this case be graded:** Aside from class participation scores, you may choose to have a case assignment that is written and graded. If you are choosing a case that will be graded, choose it with that purpose in mind. (Box Story 5)

f) **Other concerns:** At the end of the day, you need to consider where and for what reason this case is in your course.

- Lecture starter? Or heavy analysis?
- Wake People up? Give them a chance?
- What is the course content that I want to teach today? How will this case best fit?
- Should the lecture material come before or after?
- Should I include other materials during the case?
- Will this be graded as well? Assignment v. discussion?

Step 2)How long should the case last? As you think about your day of teaching, one of the first questions you need to ask is "How much time do I have, and what needs to get taught?" When you do this, you begin to understand how much time you need for lectures, course administration details (such as feedback on assignments, upcoming exams or presentations, or policy and syllabus changes) and how much time you have for the case discussion.

Even within the case, you need to make decisions on how much time you will allot to certain sections of the case. As you think about teaching the case, you might say; "I have one hour to teach the case." Once you establish that you have an hour, it helps if you can begin to organize your teaching plan to allot time for different case components. In my head I want to understand that I have roughly 10 minutes for the case introduction and synopsis, 15 minutes for the breakeven, 10 minutes to discuss the rollout plans and 5 minutes for competitive response. I want to leave 10 minutes for student questions and 5 minutes for the wrap up. While you will find it hard to be exact, it is good to have rough ideas in your head of how much time you can spend on any topic. Without a plan, you may find it hard to conclude sections of the case. But a time plan in your head forces you, as the faculty, to bring closure to the sections or components of the case.

Additionally, it is a GREAT idea to know which topics you are willing to lengthen and which you are willing to shorten, or even delete, should you get ahead or behind. It is always good to have a prioritization of the case topics in mind. If you can rank the components as "must know, good to know, and nice if you know", you have the ability to stretch or compress your case and not diminish your course objectives greatly.

Additionally, you should know which students can help you catch up if you are running behind on time. There are those students that are prone to give complete, precise, on topic, and correct answers. These are the students you would like to focus on if you are running behind, not those that are habitually wrong, incomplete in their answers an are prone to go off on tangents (more will be said about this later). Perhaps it is better to solicit answers from this latter group when you are running far ahead of your expectations and you need to fill a bit of time and give those students some encouragement. To develop, they also need their opportunities to speak in class, just perhaps not today.

Step 3) **What will be my first question? And, who should get it?** The first question has a lot to do with the tone and the direction that the case will take. This question can help you to speed the case up or slow it down. It also can have a major impact on your class dynamics and your ability to include diverse sets of people into the discussion. It is hence only appropriate that we spend a bit of time discussing impact on these three areas — tone, speed and class culture — and we will do so in reverse order

Class Culture

The first question, and whom you choose to answer it, can have a great deal of impact on how your class develops and who participates. It can be used for a variety of purposes and framed to accomplish the following goals:

A) The question as a reward or an encouragement;

a. If you are teaching an introductory or core class, many of the students may not want to be in the class and they may just be waiting for it to end each day. Furthermore, given that the class is required, they may not agree with or been keen on the case based methodology. Core instructors find that large portions of their classes don't have any desire or interest to speak up. This opening question is your opportunity to bring them aboard and allow them to contribute in a very low effort sort of manner. Simple, open and easy questions spread around to those students that are reluctant to participate can bring up their level of contribution. Examples of some such broad and vague questions that your low "participators" can easily handle include the likes of: What are some of the issues in this case? How is this company doing?

Such questions don't require extensive calculations, but rather allow the students to demonstrate their understanding of the issues, and their general understanding of the case facts. This allows them to ease their way into the class. Getting them talking is a first step in getting them interested. For many less confident students it is a way to bring them up the participation wall.

b. Many foreign or second language students have a hard time translating the past comments, formulating questions or answers, and getting their hand up in time to participate. Unlike the student that does not want to participate, these students may want to be involved but the speed and different pronunciations compromise their ability to engage. Throwing soft toss questions to them in the early part of the class helps them to participate and lets them know that they are not just forgotten in the classroom.

c. When you are trying to ensure that weaker or less participative students get involved, you may even choose to tell them they will be opening the next case. Close your lecture by saying, "We did not get Ravi, Mina, Cheng or Koh involved in class today. I want you four to be ready to open the next class." This heads-up keeps from compounding a problem of stage fright. If you call on them and they are unprepared, you may drive them deeper into a shell of non-responsiveness. Giving them a gentle heads up helps prepare them for their opportunity that will be coming in the future.

B) **The question as a punishment:** Sometimes you want to penalize a student for missing class or some other transgression in the past such as not reading or properly preparing in a past class. The first question is a time when everyone in the class is watching and you can let everyone know that you have been paying attention and there is a cost for such transgressions.

A personal anecdote: When I am discussing a case, or even lecturing, I will often make it a point to note aloud that certain students are not in class that day. I do this in a good-natured way that lets everyone know that I am paying attention. Statements such as, "If Joe was in class today, I know he would be interested in this topic as he has commented on it before." — tells the whole class that I know

Joe is not there. And that I do care about attendance. Mean-while, everyone is probably texting Joe letting him know that I have just called him out in class!

I could just stop there and it may be enough to let people know I am watching. But in my next class, my first question goes to Joe and it is generally a fairly difficult question (how difficult the question is, is a judgment between the tone I need to set and the magnitude of the student's transgression). I will normally start by saying, "Joe, we missed you in our last class so I want to be sure we get you involved today."

I find that if I do this once or twice in a semester, no one misses my class any more. I use this same discipline process for people who did not read the last time. So if I open a case and the person says; "Sorry Prof, I did not read it" — I can assure you they will open my next case.

It is important to note that this can all be done with a smile on your face and a cavalier disposition, but the message will be received. For those that are trying to establish a greater power distance relationship, this activity can be done in a less humorous and more confronting manner.

C) **The question as a means to test student preparation:** You may want to have a series of simple first questions as a means to check who has and has not been reading and preparing. What is Person X's problem? What is the competitor trying to do? Is this firm suited for the problem ahead? Several simple questions can be asked around the classroom as a means to test preparation. These may be useful queries for helping you to grade class participation scores and justify/assign grades.

Speed

The first question has a lot to do with the amount of time you will spend on the case. Asking open-ended questions, "What is going on in this case?" allows for broad participation, but it also slows down the timing of the case. Direct and pointed questions such as, "This company is facing competition from low priced competitors as well as firms willing to offer customized offerings. How should they navigate this environment?" gets you to the heart of the issues and into the solving portion of the case discussion. In the second example you have taken away much of the "what's going on in this case?" and jumped to getting solutions. For upper division electives and skilled audiences, this is fine. However, just understanding the issues and how to identify the problems may be just as important for the early stage students.

How much time you have to dedicate to the case that day often dictates the type of question you wish to ask

Tone

As you can see from above, who gets that first question and how gentle or difficult it is, has a lot to do with how you run your class and the culture you wish to keep. The openness of your first question or the pointed demand for a specific answer can go a long way in determining how students prepare and what their stakes of entry are into the class discussion. As mentioned previously, the earlier in their education the more you want to lean toward an open and easier entry level to the discussion. The closer you get to the capstone, the more you can hold one's feet to the fire. But the demands of your institution, client or oversight board might also limit your choices. Some university administrations develop uniform classroom policies to advance a rather consistent approach towards the student's educational experience. Similarly, a certain degree programme or a client in an executive education format might request that you establish a certain tone to develop a platform for other faculty that will follow.

Step 4) How will I use the instructional technology in the classroom? How you set -up your case discussion and how you deliver it is in part dictated by the classroom facilities and technologies at your disposal. Do you have multiple boards, movable boards or boards on several of the walls? Or, as is often the case, do you have just one simple flat board in the front of the room?

Planning your case discussion and what you will use the board for takes some planning. The more that you plan your board, the more easily and flawlessly you can transition between case topics in the discussion. While you should organize based on the room conditions you face, I believe a few key tips would be useful.

1) Most of the topics that you are currently working on, you want to be working on in the front of the class. Your theories, calculations and insights should be delivered in the front. Once you have solved them or summarized them, you may move the summary to a side-board (as discussed below). But people are most focused and concentrated when they are looking ahead. The key issues should be in the middle.

2) Make sure that financial comparisons or calculations are side by side. It is easier for students to check the calculations and their differences by going left to right rather than top to bottom.

3) If you have a number of key summary issues or insights, try to put them all on one board and try to have it to one side or the other. That is, students will look ahead for the work as you are

working through the problems in front of them. But if you have several summary points, put them on the side board so that they are emphasized, visible, and also away from the clutter that is taking place with the current work. This distance is an effective way for students to remember the key learnings of the case.

4) If you are going to discuss a rather large set of case issues, say four or more, put them on a single board. Preferably, these issues should be on a board in the front of the class. Then as you choose each issue and begin working on it, the distance from that issue list to the board where you are working on solutions in the front of the room would be visibly short. Keeping this distance short tends to help the students note the integrative nature of the material. The obverse also applies. If the point or topic is tangential solve it on a side-board or in a distant place. This implicates that it is not a central issue, but a distinct point.

5) If views or opinions are very different, put them on boards as far away from each other as possible. The distance helps to accentuate the difference in opinions. Unless you are intending to compare elements side by side (then put them near each other), separating views and walking back and forth between them as you discuss can have a great impact on demonstrating to the class just how different these views are. Spatial separation has a lot to do with the students' internal organization of the material.

6) If the opinions are easily compared and not radically different, put them next to each other on the front board.

7) If you have a side-board or a flip chart that is available, consider a parking lot for your case. The parking lot is where you put case issues that you want to get to later, but they don't fit in

your discussion now. Sometimes students offer answers that you are not ready to address but you do not want to forget them. By putting them in the parking lot, it helps you to remember them, lets the student know that the point is noted and important enough for you to write it down, and also helps to let other students know where you will be going in the case at some point so they can have better prepared answers.

Step 5) **What summary points will I make?** Students don't always know what they have learned, and/or what was important for them to know. In your summary you want to ensure the learning of the day. This is your opportunity to explain it again, inform the students of what they now know, tell them why it was important, and give them advice as to how they can improve the learning or skill that they have just discussed.

Personal note: I believe that cases are a journey and that you are constantly sending the students into a forest. In the forest they thrash around, and through their work and efforts find a path out of the forest. When you complete a series of difficult analytic challenges, it is a good idea to stop in the clearing and look back at the forest. Tell the students what they learned, how well they did on the path, and that now that this part of the journey is complete, prepare them for the forest or hill that lies ahead.

Thinking about how to summarize the components of the case discussion is a key step in enhancing learning and recall for the student, demonstrating and emphasizing the importance of the material and level setting for a moment before continuing discussion.

Step 6) **What future (past) points or course concepts will this discussion help me make?** Each case is a part of a semester, or a programme's long journey. While it has its day in class, it also has its place in the learning journey. The best cases integrate with your other course materials. They also exemplify or set up past or future learning points. Stopping to inform the students how the case or the material of the case links or integrates helps them to make the learning leaps across topics, domains or functions.

Note: Faculty often worry that parts of a case repeat a learning that was advanced in a previous class. But students enjoy seeing that the concepts they have studied are important enough to be touched on more than once. Also, discussing these theories or tools in multiple cases or settings not only raises their emphasis in the student's mind, but gives them multiple opportunities to see how the theory is applied. This repeated application improves their implementation capabilities. Obviously you do not want to continuously teach the same topics, but a light recap of what they already should know and a wave toward how it is relevant again here is a useful means of reinforcing learning and relevance.

Step 7) In what order will I raise the points that are central to the case? When you think about teaching a case, you want to think through what points come in what order. We all know that we don't want the summary first, and then the introduction third or some such thing. But you do have to think about what points there are, and in what order do you want to discuss them. Do you want to get all of the issues out on the board first? Then pick them off one by one? Or, would you like to ask the students for a decision or solution to the case to start? And then begin to analyze why certain answers fall short or are better than others?

What you are teaching and what the key learnings often dictates the ordering of the topics. For example, if you are teaching marketing, you generally want to begin with some sort of discussion about the customer, or the market. Then the competitor is considered, and after that the tactical solutions become easier to address. In a similar vein, most financial cases start with, and need to answer, four questions. A) How much does this investment cost? B) How much will I get back? C) When will I get it back? Financial considerations always imply that the timing affects the valuation of a return. And D) How much risk (or certainty) is there? While these rules may vary or be violated in your field, you generally recognize that problem solving is a series of steps and they do have an order to them. So think about your order and how you will keep the students marching in that correct order.

Also, your ordering has to do with your time allotment and the possibility that you will face a compressed time issue. For instance, if the case is being discussed the day after you have returned an assignment, you may find that course administration issues cut into your case time and you may need to chop or limit a topic. At times you might teach a case over multiple days. Some topics may be needed on one day or the other.

Tip: For those of you early in your teaching career that are teaching with cases that have multiple issues, a good way to take control of the class is with your first question. Asking "What are the key issues in this case?" gives you a chance to collect the key concepts from the students. You should write them on the board and then discuss them in the order you think they should be discussed. This pause is effective for new instructors trying to be in control and not always being on their back foot. Taking topics as the students throw them out and trying to respond and organize at the same time is difficult and it gives up a great deal of your control as the agenda is being set by them. But, by transcribing their comments into points on the board you a) let the students know that their point is important, and b) have the opportunity to establish the order the points will be covered.

Step 8) What *Can I,* or *Should I,* disclose? When you begin teaching a case, you may teach it for five or ten or more years. As you teach it, you get better and better at teaching the case. You invest in a case more than probably any other single pedagogical instrument. So you want to be careful about what you share and don't share. As mentioned above, letting your complete solutions walk out of the classroom can reduce the prep done by future sets of students. It is a good idea not to put your case summary slides in your lecture handouts, as students tend to pass them from generation to generation.

Additionally, if you are the case author and you have additional details of the company or individuals being discussed, you need to recognize what you are authorized to disclose and what you are not. Ethically, you never want to disclose things that were told In confidence.

Step 9) **How much should I listen? And how much should I talk?** When you think about using a case you need to recognize that sometimes you need to use the case as a way for you to lecture. With less experienced students, they have a hard time adding to the case discussion, so as a faculty you begin to do more talking, solving and lecturing of the case. Other times, you want to see what the students know. Whether it is late in an advanced course and you are trying to discern whether or not the students have attained a level of competence, or early in their development and you are listening to their instincts and preconceptions, listening can be useful. Listening is what truly enables student-centered rather than instructor-centric education.

Listening and knowing what the students understand enables you to be either the jockey and let them run with the material, or it alerts you that you, the instructor, must supply small summaries or mini lectures to elaborate on the concepts and materials.

Step 10) **Develop a case file and keep notes.** Your case teaching is always a work in progress and you will find that if you take a few moments at the end of the class to jot down what worked and what did not work, it will help you prepare for the next time. Each time you teach a case you develop some new insights or you get a question or answer from a student that illuminates a potentially new and interesting facet of the case. Taking a moment at the end of class when it is still fresh in your mind to record or compose your thoughts will help your preparation for the next time.

Also, between teaching opportunities, you may encounter interesting information about the company featured in the case or some of the competitors or actors. Having a repository to store these interesting facts and insights will help you stay prepared, evolve in your preparation and appear more current and relevant. Bringing an article or two to the attention of the students that explains what the company has done or what it is doing today is a way to further the case epilogue. These post mortem stories can help provide richness and insights. That these articles come from a third party source bolsters the legitimacy of what the students just learned, and they tend to give the faculty high marks for their class preparation.

But for you, the teaching file is a key step in preparing each time. Writing yourself notes about what worked well (What question worked like a dream and got a great dialogue going?) and what fell with a thud (What were those questions asked that the class did not understand how to respond to or what to do, or worse yet, went in the wrong direction). Writing notes regarding what topics you should be prepared to expand or reduce, or those that can be hurried or slowed down, all give you greater teaching flexibility. You are the conductor of this symphony, a few notes about the music can go a long way in helping you lead.

Box Story 5: A Grading Recommendation

Through the years I have personally wrestled with and asked many professors what the purpose is of their grading. Seemingly an easy question, I am always surprised by how long the answers take to articulate. Moreover, the answers are often absent of what the intended academic benefits of grading are. A case is like any other assignment and if you are to grade it, you want to be sure you understand:

1) Why you are grading it?
2) What criteria will you be employing to assign the grade?
3) What feedback will you be giving?
4) How fast will you be returning the assignments
5) How can you reduce student complaints and concerns?

1) Ask yourself: "Why are you actually grading this assignment?"

   a. Is it meant to be an assessment of the student journey and the overall learning and mastery of the materials? A common purpose of written or presentation based case assignments is to see if the students are actually grasping the course concepts and if they can apply them. Cases can be an opportunity to employ cognitive problem solving skills which demonstrate greater mastery of the subjects at hand.

   b. Is the grading meant as encouragement? When teaching seemingly lengthy and complex subjects, case

---

(Continued)

(Continued)

assignments can be used to help the student learner to understand just how far they have progressed in their competency. Such revelations can be encouraging and also serve as a source of confidence for future success.

c. At times, grading a case is used to give closure to a course, a module, or a topic.

2) What criteria will you be employing to grade the case?
   As a start, you want to be sure that if students are to complete an assignment, they have the format that you require for the final work product. This helps the students to comply, and it makes your grading more efficient. It should include what might be the headings, the expected length of each section, even the types of concepts that should be addressed in each of the sections. Below, in Exhibit A, a very simple potential written rubric is demonstrated. This guide for writing up a case helps to make your grading easier and more efficient, as the student work is more readily comparable.

   a. If you can, let the students know how you will weigh the sub sections of the assignment.

   b. Students will always want to know what will win out. Will there be higher marks for creativity, precision, rigor, balanced arguments, critical insights, thoroughness, or employing course materials? It is important to inform students what you will emphasis in your grading.

(Continued)

(Continued)

3) What feedback do you intend to provide. Feedback on graded work is one of the great opportunities for student learning. This is sometimes a tricky decision. You want the student to understand what they did wrong, but you don't want to provide such a detailed solution that it is easy for other classes in the future to get a hold of the "answer key" you have provided and simply copy it. Thus it is highly recommended that you provide simple calculations on the student paper at specific points rather than a single detailed solution at the end of the paper. This is really a decision regarding how much is enough, and how much is too much.

A second consideration has to do with the tone you want to take on your grading. Usually it is a good idea to tell the students initially about the positives that they showed in their work. This lets them know that you have read their work and reduces many comments and re-grading requests as they believe the score is more just and comprehensive. It has been robustly demonstrated that students are less likely to complain about their grades when the professor has made specific positive references to their work.

How you deliver negative feedback is up to you, but several rules should be observed:

a. Do not personalize the comments. Instead of saying, "You did this wrong or that wrong", it is better to refer to third parties. "If management did this, they would quickly find that the competitor had a lower cost structure and

(Continued)

(*Continued*)

they might find a response based on price sparking lower margins in the industry...." Such comments depersonalize the feedback.

b. Early in the semester it is best to have gentle feedback. "This is a great job of identifying the problem. What would have made this a fantastic answer is if there had been a recommended solution for how to solve this problem. Good managers don't just spot the problem, they solve it." Such a comment is depersonalized, points out the positive and lets the student know that the error is in not providing prescriptive steps.

c. Think about how your feedback can help them do better in the future. Making references to how they should have handled a question and how in the future they will need to understand, recognize and employ certain logics, is very helpful in improving student work.

Feedback on graded work is one of the great opportunities for student learning. It deserves your consideration as to how you want to deliver the messages and when. But this is probably one of the most student-centric parts of teaching. Thinking about how, when, and in what format, you want to deliver feedback is a key decision

4) When you will deliver feedback and grades is an important decision. I personally recommend that you never give an assignment until you have had the time to grade it. Immediate impact is most useful and instructive for the

(*Continued*)

(Continued)

students. So, it is important to return assignments in a timely manner.

Let's be honest! As a professor, most of us dislike grading and we all dislike the students' looks and complaints that we get when we give them back their papers. Sure the first five papers are illuminating as you learn what you did or did not teach well. But the next 60 papers are sheer misery. Probably the only thing I hate more than the grading process is the thought of knowing that I have to grade.

Personally, if students take my exam at 6 pm, I return the papers in their mailbox before they arrive at school the next morning. Gathering my electronic files before a long plane flight and grading case assignments on the aircraft is a way to reduce the stress of travel and the stress of having to grade. As I said, give assignments when you have the time to grade them.

Rule of thumb: Grade it now, not later. The opportunity for learning decays dramatically with time, so grade it soon.

5) How can I reduce student complaints? Student complaints can be reduce greatly if you think about how to properly message the feedback you will give. Remember they have put in a herculean effort (or so they claim) and bared their thoughts on this paper. They are invested and vulnerable. You need to think about how to get the message across that they have not fully reached your expectations, but you want them to be encouraged to try again.

(Continued)

(Continued)

a. Again, elaborate on their positives. It encourages, and it shows that you have listened.

b. Think about how you want to deliver class statistics. Do you want to disclose the class grade range? I remember working as a TA and a faculty member told me, "I always report the lowest grade 5 points lower than my lowest actual score. The student that gets the lowest grade, or for that matter those very close to last, will be upset not just with themselves but me as a teacher."

c. Can you still achieve a grade distribution while giving acceptable raw scores? Another professor told me, "Grade all the questions from 50–100%. If they write down anything, in essence they are getting a minimum of 50% partial credit. That halts most complaints. In the end we will assign final grades on a 50–100 scale."

d. Provide an exemplar or two of good work. Clip a paragraph or table from a past semester of what you consider to be high quality work and insert it in their paper. This longer and elaborate feedback reduces complaints.

Chapter 5

PERFORMING/DELIVERY

How you deliver is in large part a question of style and what you are comfortable with. Do I want to be friendly or a harsh taskmaster? Do I want slow and thoughtful discussions holding a limited number of students accountable for significant participation, or do I want quick-paced on your toes interchanges where many students get involved? These questions are up to you to answer and they partially depend on the subject, class size and student background.

Just how you execute your classroom plan is up to you, but there are a few ground rules that you need to keep in mind.

1) **You OWN the room!**
   You may be teaching for the benefit of the students but it is your stage and you have the pulpit in your hands. So,

   - You determine the emphasis
   - You determine who speaks
   - You determine who does *not* speak
   - You determine the tone or personality of the class
   - You determine the ENERGY

- You determine the pace
- You determine the culture
- It is up to you.......

a. Emphasis: What topics will be discussed and for how long is largely up to you, the instructor, and what you wish to cover. Students can ask questions, but how long you wish to spend on any topic or any question for that matter is up to you. Recognizing that you control the agenda is a powerful realization. It also must be used properly as you want to allot your time properly to cover the important points.

b. As discussed earlier, you determine who does or does not get to speak in class. Whether you wish to grant air time to students — to encourage, punish, challenge, enrich or demonstrate balance — you are in control. Who you choose and why tells the class a lot about the rules of the game. When students miss your class, calling on them first and letting them know that you want to give them the opportunity to be involved as they were not in your last class lets them know a lot about the rules of your classroom. Similarly, for those that were unprepared, calling on them again in the next class is a signal that you are checking.

c. Who does not speak is also an intentional decision on your part. Often you have students that give crisp and precise answers. When you are running behind, you want to choose them. On the other hand there are students that really don't understand the course or the subject matter. Their hand being up in the air is often less of a signal that they have an answer than a sign that they have a question. At times, you venture into such waters and spend the time in the open tutorial of the classroom. At other times you just have to avoid them. Similarly, you begin to realize that some students are one-trick ponies and will continuously ask for applications to a single industry or functional area. If you have neither the answers nor the desire to answer such questions, avoid them.

d. The class personality is largely yours to establish. If you want a loose class, engage them loosely and encourage them to elaborate on answers. If you want an intense class, make them give you precise answers and continue to drill down on the student to supply logic. The first method will encourage all to be and feel a part of the class. The latter may discourage students from offering their opinions without being called on. Thus you will have to do more cold-calling in the latter case than in the first.

e. Energy is something you can always establish in the classroom. I like a high energy class and each day I enter welcoming the students *to day number "X" of the most exciting topic in business today*. While I may not always be excited to be in the classroom, stating this and trying to deliver on it keeps an energy and an intensity in the class that might not otherwise exist.

f. Along with energy, you establish the pace. How fast after the last answer you ask for a follow-up response, or how long you will wait for a student to answer before calling on another, provides cues as to your pace and the appropriate timing. If you still want to have a student involved but they have taken too long to answer, tell them I will come back to you in a few minutes on topic X. This can also help students with language challenges to be able to respond in an appropriate time period, rather than having to amend your style greatly.

g. The culture, much like the pace and energy, is yours to establish. If you want the students to be critical of each other, pit one against another. Ask the student what is wrong with the other students' answers. If you want to soften that, ask them what alternative theories or prescriptive steps might be taken? And if you want to create a least threatening environment, keep asking them how the protagonists in the case might have done things differently. The same questions asked somewhat differently create a very different environment.

The classroom is yours as the instructor. Recognizing that you have the power to shape it is the first step in properly delivering.

2) Never panic

Even if you don't know the answer to a question, it is not really a problem. Stop, think about it, and throw it out to the room. Let the students supply you with answers. If you still do not feel you have a proper answer, let the students work on it between classes as you prepare for the next class. And it is not always a bad idea to acknowledge that it is a worthwhile topic but you don't have a definite answer at this time. This often demonstrates that you will do the work to respond to, and prepare for, student questions. But be sure to come back to it in the future class.

3) Be human in the classroom

Yes, students like to see that their professor is larger than life. But, they also have more empathy for you when you humanize your stories. If you are teaching a point on customer service, provide them an example of when you faced it. Students like to know that what you experience is much like what they experience. This sort of connection helps the faculty to avoid the "irrelevance" refrain from the chorus of discontented students.

4) Relate the cases to the student's life
The fact that a faculty is in touch with the popular culture, or the student's life, helps to establish relevance and is always appreciated by the class. There are several ways to bring simple connections between yourself and the students. These connections help you to personalize your materials.

   a. Understand what is happening in their lives. Students are often going through a semester cycle. They have a period of exams, or job interviews or even social events that are at the top of their mind. Stop and ask: how would knowing this help you in a job interview? Or as you prepare for the exam in class X, you may want to consider this. Just the fact that you are letting students know that you understand what is going on in their life helps them to gain confidence that you are aware of the situation and thus reasonable in your expectations.

   b. Can you relate the material to specific experiences in a students' life. If you do know where they are from, where they have worked, what their hobbies are, you have all sorts of opportunities to customize your questions. Instead of asking: "What did the case protagonist do?", you can follow up or ask: "John, when you worked at XYZ, did you ever witness people behaving this way?" This tells students that you think about them, and you take an interest in their lives.

   c. A simple look at the paper or a review of socially relevant online sights like the most viewed YouTube videos or the campus newspaper often provides the opportunity for you to connect your material.

5) Watch your pace

There is no prize for speed. While I personally like a fast moving class, remember you do not have to rush to answer questions. Inexperienced faculty can sometimes be a bit nervous. In their anxiety, they look to rush through questions and answers or speak quite hurriedly. Instead of accepting a partial answer from a student and then asking others to add to the point or comment on what is said, they begin solving the points themselves. This can shut down a very key skill development that the case method is striving for. The discussion-based pedagogy allows the students to reason with the comments that are made and try to improve them and fit them into their logic. This processing of information in a real time setting provides the opportunity to take ownership of the material. Just remember to stop and slowdown from time to time.

6) Be flexible

Remember the students are not machines. They just return from holidays, they have end of quarter work commitments, the other instructors are giving midterm exam or assigning papers. Acknowledge that you are aware of this, and let them know that you expect more in the future. *"Today, I realize I can't get blood from a stone! But next time you better be ready to participate...."* These sort of statements allow for connections.

Some Tips for Handling Common Classroom Problems

Each time you teach your class is a bit different, but there are common difficulties and challenges that we all run into quite frequently. Below is a list of some of the more frequently encountered problems that my colleagues have expressed to me over the years. As we discussed these, I have included some of their solutions and thoughts.

Students that are Rude

Generally, I do not escalate, even if I am seething inside, as if students see me losing my temper, the entire class gets disturbed. I try and use humor and put the student down gently, saying that I would have made the same point in a different way, but we all have our personalities. If the student is persistently rude, this is the only case where I get confrontational, and tell the student that this behavior will not be tolerated, etc. As a rule of thumb, I would advise professors never to lose their temper, as it would mean they lose control of the class as well. In some cases it is unavoidable, but then the class understands the predicament I am in. If this does happen, the students generally tell off the rude student as well.

Shantanu Bhattacharya, Professor of Operations at SMU and formerly INSEAD nominee for best core professor

The Question I Can't Answer

I will generally be upfront that I do not know the answer to the question, and state the reasons for me not knowing the answer. However, I rarely leave a question unanswered. I say clearly that my answer is a conjecture, but here are my thoughts, and then I share my thoughts on the question. In most cases no one knows the right answer with a complete confidence level in the business world, but we have to play the percentages in our decisions. Letting the students witness my spontaneous logic often helps them to gain confidence and practice into how they can participate in a management setting even if they do not know the answers with perfect confidence.

— Rajendra K. Srivastava, Dean Indian School of Business

The Student that won't keep Quiet

It seems that there is often a student that will continuously com-ment on every topic and discussion in the class. This monopolizing of the class discussion is often distracting to the instructor and annoying to the class participants. When I asked faculty about this problem, they all wanted to answer. So let me provide a few of their insights.

a) *I try to slow them down in class by not calling on them each time. But if they persist in butting into the discussion, I generally have a word with them outside of class and thank them for their efforts and insights, and explain to them that while I appreciate their energy and comments I will only be calling on them when I need them. I explain that they have already done enough on their class participation and that their grades will not be negatively impacted by my decision to call on others.*

— *Siddharth S. Singh Ph.D., Professor of Marketing, Indian School of Business*

b) *In general, if one student is hogging the limelight, I have a cas-caded approach to deal with it. In my experience, usually humor works. I first say that all students deserve a chance at class partici-pation, and XYZ has already scored 20 out of 10 on class participa-tion. If the student is socially challenged and will not take a hint, I go to the next level, and do not ask for this student's comment even if his/her hand is raised. And if this student speaks out of turn, I gently reprimand him/her by saying that we all should get our say in the conversation, and s/he had plenty of turns already. I have yet to come across a student who escalates further, but I guess I would then have to firmly tell the student not to disturb the class further.*

— *Shantanu Bhattacharya Ph.D., Singapore Management University)*

c) Personally, I always found that avoiding eye contact and using your body to limit their access to discussion can be helpful. I will generally walk to where that student is and turn my back towards them and face another set of the class as I call for an answer. The fact that they can't gain access to my vision may be frustrating, but it will temporarily limit this issue.

Students that talk to each other while the case discussion is on

This is probably one of the most annoying characteristics. As a young instructor, you immediately start thinking that they are confused with your concepts or they are talking about something you are doing wrong. There are several low risk ways to handle this problem

a) You can stop talking and focus on the students waiting for them to stop talking. This interruption of the class is generally sufficient to send the message to all that there will only be one conversation at a time.

b) *I generally stop and directly ask them if there is something that they don't understand. If that is the case they let me know. If it isn't they generally get the hint.*

— *Eyal Maoz, Ph.D., Associate Dean for Teaching and Curriculum, Ono College*

c) *I will ask them: "Hey we all are a bit bored here also, why don't you share the joke with us?" I say this with a smile and the class will generally laugh but everyone seems to comply.*

— *Pannapachr Itthiopassagul, Director Master's Degree Program in Marketing, Thammasat University, Thailand*

The Comment that is Not on Point

This is a question too that got many answers from my peers. They ranged from asking the student to repeat their answer, to asking the student the same question and asking them to try to answer again, to simply saying "Let us just move on" — which lets the student know they have grossly missed the point.

Personally I have found that if I rephrase the student's answer they will generally agree with it. For example if they say "I would do it", I would rephrase and say "So are you advocating that with sales forecasts of X and the competitive entry of firm Z and the impending regulations that you would still launch this product?" This rephrasing helps the whole class to gain the pertinent facts, and presents the student with a digestible question to which they can offer a simple answer.

Students that Enter Class Late

Some instructors say they don't care, others employ a grading policy that reduces student grades for being tardy, or they have a meeting with the student during the break. Personally, I find it difficult to begin a case discussion when people are entering class late. So what works for you may vary depending on your level of frustration.

Perhaps one of the most powerful examples I have come across is that of Sundar Bhardwaj (Professor, The University of Georgia). When students were late to his class. Dr Bhardwaj would stop talking and stare at the student from the time he/she entered the classroom until the moment they sat down. This focused attention begets the attention of the student and all of his/her classroom peers. This public scrutiny is generally enough to limit the behavior by all.

Students that do not Attend Class

There are a variety of ways to promote attendance. Tying grades to in class attendance and performance is the most direct route. But there are also several ways to keep the students from ditching your class.

a) When you begin class, take a mental note as to who is missing that day. As the lecture or case discussion moves along, simply state that if say, Peter, was here today, he would be very interested in this topic. It is a shame he is not here. You can be quite sure that before the next class, Peter will be contacting you to explain his absence!

b) A similar approach is to wait until the class next meets. Simply start the class with Peter. You may even let him know that the reason he is being called on is that we want to be sure to get his participation while he is here. How difficult you make this opening can do a great deal to establish better attendance and create a culture.

These are a few of the common problems that all faculty struggle through in trying to conduct their symphony in the classroom. Every class is different as is every instructor. It is best if you think about what works for you and what style you want to adopt. Taskmaster? Cheerleader? Conductor? Facilitator? Friendly mentor? Or the Devil's Advocate? The choice is yours as you own the room.

Chapter 6

CONCLUSION

I hope that the 5 chapters of this book and the insights shared by my colleagues were useful to the readers. Teaching is a skill like many others. To improve as a case teacher, requires practice, analysis, introspection and a keen desire to improve. The best case teachers tend to be the people that search out other great teachers, attend their classes and put themselves in situations that challenge them.

When I began teaching I started tutoring a group of second language Japanese students at Northwestern University. The students were bright, attentive and came prepared every day. But they struggled with the language. My challenge as a teacher was how to pick common words that they could understand when I spoke, to speak in a slow pace and to be sure that my sentences were short enough for the meanings to be translated. These sort of teaching challenges will be a bit trying but they will make you a better teacher. Learning to be precise, exact and economical in your communication is a great start to being effective.

As one develops throughout their teaching career they transition from lecturer to facilitator to coach and possibly to mentor. As you grow as a teacher, look to vary your audience level as quickly as you can. Teach executives or masters level students and encourage them to add to your class discussion. The more levels that you teach at, the more you understand the general level of understanding of the material you teach. Teaching at different levels helps you to develop an accordion approach to your stories and examples. Knowing how to expand or explain them at the most micro of levels, or how to quickly condense the story into a high level narrative provides you with great flexibility in the classroom.

Try to teach several industry specific programmes. Often it is when you try to teach the same material to a vastly different group that you begin to find new ways to relate, explain and connect your questions, materials and lectures.

Most of all, I hope that you had fun reading this book and that you will enjoy your opportunities to instruct with cases. If you follow some of the tips in this book and approach each class as a learning opportunity where you have an opportunity to learn how to better teach your content, you will continuously improve. The more that you record, review and make notes about your experiences the faster your teaching will improve and the more you will enjoy this part of the profession.

In my nearly 30 years of teaching I have found that cases have been nearly as enriching to me as they are for the students. Each time I teach a case I hear a unique insight or a novel comment that stimulates my own analysis. It is this sort of feedback loop that helps us to grow as faculty and to deepen our understanding.

EXHIBIT A: A SIMPLE GUIDE TO HOW TO WRITE UP YOUR CLASS ASSIGNMENTS CASES

Writing up a case. In the formal write-up, use the following headings:

1. Purpose of the Report

State the purpose of the report. Specify the problems to be addressed in your analysis. The firm has retained you to assist them in handling certain problems. State the problems you will be solving. This is often called an executive summary of the issues at hand.

2. Option Listing

List the potential options that are available to the organization or actor in the case. In example, the firm could

A) embark upon strategy X,
B) The management could choose to execute on Strategy Y.
C) Management could postpone their decision and review at a later time or,
D) They could do nothing.

3. Recommendations

Tell me what course you recommend and why. State the manner in which each of the problems you have identified should be resolved. In this section, only your recommendations should be given. Reasons for the recommendations should appear in the analysis.

3. Analysis

This is the heart of your report. It entails marshaling factual data which can support your problem identification and your recommended course of action. In essence, it is the link between problem and recommendations. No solution comes without problems or opportunities. State the manner in which each of the problems you have identified should be resolved. For example, if the first issue you address in your analysis is the target audience, use target audience as a side heading. If the next issue is creative strategy, use it as a side heading.

4. Summary

This summary is an opportunity for you to repeat your arguments in a clear and logical manner to ensure that the reader understand your problem identification, proposed solutions, course of action and the justification for this decision.

Printed in the United States
By Bookmasters